DALLEY
AND THE MALAYAN SECURITY SERVICE, 1945-48

The **ISEAS – Yusof Ishak Institute** (formerly Institute of Southeast Asian Studies) is an autonomous organization established in 1968. It is a regional centre dedicated to the study of socio-political, security, and economic trends and developments in Southeast Asia and its wider geostrategic and economic environment. The Institute's research programmes are grouped under Regional Economic Studies (RES), Regional Strategic and Political Studies (RSPS), and Regional Social and Cultural Studies (RSCS). The Institute is also home to the ASEAN Studies Centre (ASC), the Nalanda-Sriwijaya Centre (NSC) and the Singapore APEC Study Centre.

ISEAS Publishing, an established academic press, has issued more than 2,000 books and journals. It is the largest scholarly publisher of research about Southeast Asia from within the region. ISEAS Publishing works with many other academic and trade publishers and distributors to disseminate important research and analyses from and about Southeast Asia to the rest of the world.

DALLEY
AND THE MALAYAN SECURITY SERVICE, 1945–48

MI5 VS. MSS

LEON COMBER

ISEAS YUSOF ISHAK INSTITUTE

First published in Singapore in 2019 by
ISEAS Publishing
30 Heng Mui Keng Terrace
Pasir Panjang
Singapore 119614

Email: publish@iseas.edu.sg
Website: <http://bookshop.iseas.edu.sg>

All rights reserved. No part of this publication may be reproduced, stored in a retrieval system, or transmitted in any form or by any means, electronic, mechanical, photocopying, recording or otherwise, without the prior permission of the Institute of Southeast Asian Studies.

© 2019 ISEAS – Yusof Ishak Institute, Singapore

The responsibility for facts and opinions in this publication rests exclusively with the author and his interpretations do not necessarily reflect the views or the policy of the publisher or its supporters.

ISEAS Library Cataloguing-in-Publication Data

Comber, Leon, 1921–
Dalley and the Malayan Security Service, 1945–48 : MI5 vs. MSS
1. Dalley, John Douglas—1900–
2. Intelligence service—Malaya—History—Malayan Emergency, 1948–1960.
3. Internal security—Malaya.
4. National security—Malaya.
I. Title.
DS596.5 C721   2019

ISBN 978-981-4818-73-5 (soft cover)
ISBN 978-981-4818-74-2 (e-book, PDF)

Typeset by Superskill Graphics Pte Ltd
Printed in Singapore by Mainland Press Pte Ltd

CONTENTS

Preface vii

Acknowledgements xiii

List of Abbreviations xv

1. Lieutenant Colonel John Dalley and the MSS: Early Days 1

2. Lieutenant Colonel John Dalley and Dalforce 13

3. The Establishment of "Security Intelligence Far East (SIFE)" in Singapore 35

4. Dalley's Return to Singapore 45

5. The Indonesian Situation and Malaya 56

6. Indonesian Encroachment into Malaya 88

7. Arrangements for Allocation of MSS Staff to Special Branch, Singapore, and Special Branch, Malaya 99

8. Conclusion 104

Appendix 1. Diagram of Communist & Left-wing Malayan and Indonesian Political Movements, PIJ 1948 108

Appendix 2. A Review of Malayan Communist Party Policy, PIJ 1948 110

Bibliography 139

Index 147

About the Author 157

PREFACE

This book is the result of a conversation I had with the late Mr S.R. Nathan, the distinguished former President of Singapore, whom I had first known in Johor Baru where he was working for the Public Works Department (PWD) before he moved to Singapore and eventually became President of Singapore. I was then in the Johor Special Branch. Much later, when he moved to Singapore and became President, and I was no longer a Special Branch officer but had become a Visiting Senior Fellow at ISEAS – Yusof Ishak Institute, Singapore, we renewed our acquaintance and we used to meet sometimes, at his invitation, in his office at the Singapore Istana to discuss intelligence matters in which, having been at one time Director of the Security and Intelligence Division of the Singapore Ministry of Defence before he became President, he maintained a keen interest.

He knew that I had written a book on the Malayan Special Branch,[1] and he asked why I did not write a similar study about the Malayan Security Service (MSS), which was the domestic intelligence agency established by the British covering both Singapore and Malaya from its headquarters in Singapore when they returned to Singapore after the Japanese surrender in August 1945. When I said I was interested, he arranged for me to be allowed to use the digitized records of the MSS that were held by Singapore's ISD (Internal Security Department) in the ISD

Heritage Centre, Onraet Road. It was then I started my research on this book, *Dalley and the Malayan Security Service, 1945–48: MI5 vs. MSS*, although as I explained to Mr Nathan, I would perhaps sometimes have to rely on some of the background material I had used in my earlier paper "The Malayan Security Service (1945–1948)"[2] and book *Malaya's Secret Police 1945–60: The Role of the Special Branch in the Malayan Emergency*,[3] although I would incorporate in my present writing, wherever necessary, further information and insights which had come to light since then.

In writing this study, full use has therefore been made of the fortnightly reports of the MSS's *Political and Security Journal* (*PIJ*) and its *Supplements*, complete runs of which have been digitized and held in the ISD, which I did not have access to when I wrote about the MSS so many years ago.[4]

Perhaps it may be of interest at this stage to record the earliest post-WWII mention of the MSS, which appeared in Serial No. 1/1946 of the MSS's *Political Intelligence Journal*, dated 30 April 1946, which relates to MSS's position as a combined Singapore/Malayan political/security intelligence organization, with its headquarters in Singapore:

Note on MSS Organisation

At present temporarily on a pan-Malayan basis, pending a final decision by the two Malayan governments, the MSS is responsible for civil security intelligence throughout the country. Proposed that HQ should be in Singapore, with a sub-headquarters office in Kuala Lumpur and branches in Singapore, Selangor (to include Negri Sembilan, Perak South, and Pahang), Penang (to include Province Wellesley, Kedah, Perlis and Perak North), Johor (including Malacca) and Kelantan (to include Terengganu).

> Owing to shortage of officers the organisation is at present operating on skeleton framework, with officers in Singapore, Kuala Lumpur, Johor Baru, Penang and Alor Star.
>
> [The] Journal is [a] successor of [the] *Political Intelligence Journal* previously published by Special Branch, Singapore, C.I.B. (Political) Kuala Lumpur, and the office of the Civil Security Officer Malaya.

However, in addition to the important *PIJ* files of the MSS available at the ISD Heritage Centre, it has been necessary, too, in order to obtain a broader picture of the intelligence canvas, to carry out additional research relating to intelligence matters held for the relevant period in (a) the National Archives of Singapore (NAS); (b) Arkib Negara Kuala Lumpur; (c) the Australian National Archives (ANA), Canberra; and (d) archival documents ordered by the ISEAS – Yusof Ishak Institute Library from the Public Records Office, Kew, that I had not seen before, for which the author is grateful, such as DVD FCO 15 141/14360, "Singapore: Pan Malayan Security Service Security Intelligence Far East (SIFE)" (1946 Jan 01–1946 Dec 31); DVD FCO 15 141/16880, "Singapore: Internal Security in Malaya" (1946 Jan 01–1947 Dec 31); and DVD FCO 15 KV 4/423 "Organisation and Functions of Security Intelligence Far East (SIFE)" (1948 Oct 07–1949 May 14).

There is a little information, too, but only on the fringes of the topic I am dealing with, in some of the following reports for the period:

(a) Malayan Weekly Situation Telegrams
(b) Malayan Weekly Police Summaries
(c) Monthly Chinese Affairs Reports
(d) FARELF (Far East Land Forces) Reports

(e) Malayan Monthly Chinese/Malay/Tamil Press Summaries
(f) Malayan Monthly Political Reports from Federation of Malaya
(g) Monthly Political Reports from Singapore.

In more recent times, further interest has been shown in the MSS since the author's earlier contributions by Roger Arditti and Philip H.J. Davies in their "Rethinking the Rise and Fall of the Malayan Security Service, 1946–48" (2014),[5] Arditti's PhD thesis "Our Achilles Heel — Interagency Intelligence during the Malayan Emergency" (2015),[6] and Alexander Nicholas Shaw's "MI5 and the Cold War in South-East Asia: Examining the Performance of Security Intelligence Far East (SIFE), 1946–1963" (2017),[7] which are useful and add to our knowledge of the MSS.

Perhaps it may be pertinent, however, at this stage to say a few words about the above studies before passing on to the present concern of this book, which focuses on Dalley and the MSS.

While Arditti and Davies's excellent paper does mention Lai Teck, the Secretary General of the Malayan Communist Party (MCP),[8] they do not bring out that he had actually been a Singapore Special Branch (SB) "double agent" supplying information to the Singapore SB since pre-war days — in fact, in his time he had been a "triple agent" employed consecutively by the French, British, and Japanese secret services. He was, too, one of MSS's primary sources of human intelligence during Dalley's time. There is no doubt, however, that his absconding with the MCP's funds in March 1947 must have resulted in the loss of an important source of inside information about the MCP and its operations.

Referring further to "Rethinking the Rise and Fall of the Malayan Security Service, 1946–48", and "Dalley's return to Malaya at the end of 1946", actually, Dalley returned to Singapore on 5 February 1947, and there is a photograph of him in the

Straits Times of 6 February 1947 taken immediately after he had disembarked from the ship that had carried him from the UK to Singapore, where he gathered around him some of his supporters to address them.

Referring to footnote 82 in Arditti and Davies's paper concerning the title used for MSS officers, perhaps it should be brought out that the authority for the use of the term "Local Security Officers" (LSO) to indicate MSS officers is to be found in the official Colonial Office *Malayan Establishment List*.

The MSS posted an LSO to each of the Malay States except for Kelantan, Terengganu, Melaka and Pahang, where it was prevented from doing so by a shortage of staff. However, in these four states, arrangements were made for the relevant state Criminal Investigation Department (CID) to cover intelligence matters for the MSS. Although it may not have been completely satisfactory, it was better than nothing.

Perhaps Roger Christopher Arditti could have mentioned in his PhD, too, that the Malayan Special Branch was often used with the uniformed branch of the police in an infantry role to fight the MCP's jungle army for the first year or so of the First Malayan Emergency (1948–60), when there were insufficient army units on the ground in Malaya to counter the uprising. Clearly this must have had a serious effect on the provision of intelligence until at least army reinforcements arrived from the UK and various parts of the British Empire, such as Hong Kong, Australia, New Zealand and Fiji, which enabled the Special Branch to revert to its normal function of providing operational intelligence.

Notes

1. Leon Comber, *Malaya's Secret Police 1945–1960: The Role of the Special Branch in the Malayan Emergency* (Singapore: Institute of Southeast Asian Studies/Monash University Press, 2008).

2. Leon Comber, "The Malayan Security Service (1945–1948)", *Intelligence and National Security* 18, no. 3 (Autumn 2003): 128–53.
3. Comber, *Malaya's Secret Police*.
4. Some copies of the *PIJ* are held in CO 537/3751 and CO 537/3753 but they do not appear to be complete runs and not all the Supplements are attached.
5. Roger Arditti and Philip H.J. Davies, "Rethinking the Rise and Fall of the Malayan Security Service, 1946–48", *Journal of Imperial and Commonwealth History* 43, no. 2 (2014): 292–316.
6. Roger Christopher Arditti, "Our Achilles Heel — Interagency Intelligence during the Malayan Emergency" (PhD dissertation, Brunel Centre for Intelligence and Security Studies, September 2015).
7. Alexander Nicholas Shaw, "MI5 and the Cold War in South-East Asia: Examining the Performance of Security Intelligence Far East (SIFE), 1946–1963", *Intelligence and National Security* 32, no. 6 (2017): 797–816.
8. Arditti and Davies, "Rethinking the Rise and Fall", pp. 302–3.

ACKNOWLEDGEMENTS

I am grateful to Director Choi Shing Kwok and Senior Advisor Tan Chin Tiong of my home institute, the ISEAS – Yusof Ishak Institute, for their cooperation and provision of facilities for the writing of the book as a Visiting Senior Fellow at ISEAS.

I wish to acknowledge the great encouragement, help and advice I have always received from the late President of Singapore, Mr S.R. Nathan, in his office at ISEAS and over several meetings held in his office at the Singapore Istana, in researching and writing the book. It was through his recommendation I was able to obtain permission to research the digitized material on the Malayan Security Service held at the ISD Heritage Centre.

I wish to acknowledge, too, the assistance and cooperation I have always received from Kenneth Foo, Raymond Ng, Wee Chin and Joshua Chee on my visits to the ISD Heritage Centre to research the digitized MSS files which are held there, and for the hospitality they have always extended to me on my visits.

My thanks are due, too, to Lin Chung Ying, Special Assistant, National Security Coordinating Secretariat (NSCS), Prime Minister's Office, for his much appreciated help in obtaining photos for the book.

Ng Kok Kiong, Head of ISEAS Publishing and its Managing Editor, and his Senior Editor Rahilah Yusof and Stephen Logan,

Editor – Special Projects, have all provided me with greatly valued help in technical publishing matters connected with the book.

My debt to Lee Su Yin, an outstanding educator, historian, and an author in her own right, is immeasurable. Throughout the research and writing of the book, I cannot speak too highly of her unstinting collaboration and help in many ways. Her comments were always of the greatest value and without her advice this study could not have been completed.

ABBREVIATIONS

API	Angkatan Pemuda Indonesia (Enlighted Youth League)
ASP	Assistant Superintendent of Police
BAM	British Association of Malaya
BMA	British Military Administration
CCP	Chinese Communist Party
CDL	China Democratic League
CID	Criminal Investigation Department
CO	Colonial Office
DSO	Defence Security Officer
GLU	General Labour Union
GOC	General Officer Commanding
IGP	Inspector General of Police
ISD	Internal Security Department
KMM	Kesatuan Melayu Muda (Malay Youth Union)
LSO	Local Security Officer
MCA	Malayan Chinese Association
MCP	Malayan Communist Party
MCS	Malayan Civil Service
MIC	Malayan Indian Congress
MNP	Malay Nationalist Party
MPAJA	Malayan People's Anti-Japanese Army
MSS	Malayan Security Service
NDYL	New Democratic Youth League

OCPD	Officer-in-Charge, Police District
PAP	People's Action Party
PARI	Partai Republican Indonesia
PETA	Ikatan Pemudah Tanah Ayer (Youth Defence Corps.)
PIJ	*Political Intelligence Journal*
RAF	Royal Air Force
SB	Special Branch
SEAC	South East Asia Command
SFTU	Singapore Federation of Trade Unions
SHLU	Singapore Harbour Labour Union
SID	Security and Intelligence Division
SIFE	Security Intelligence Far East
UMNO	United Malays National Organisation
WFDY	World Federation of Democratic Youth Convention
WFTU	World Federation of Trade Unions

Chapter 1

Lieutenant Colonel John Dalley and the MSS: Early Days

Who was Lieutenant Colonel John Douglas Dalley, Director of the Malayan Security Service (MSS), and what was the MSS?

Dalley was a senior pre-war officer of the Malayan Police who became Commander of Dalforce (named after him), an irregular guerrilla force that fought bravely against the Japanese when they invaded Malaya/Singapore in 1941, and later became Director MSS. An account of Dalforce will be given later in this study.

Dalley joined the Federated Malay States Police as a Cadet Assistant Superintendent of Police in November 1920 when he was twenty. That was the average age for Malayan/Singapore police gazetted officers to join the Malayan Police at that rank. After passing in due course the required Malayan Government examinations for gazetted police officers in police law, colonial regulations, Malayan Government regulations, weapon training and Malay language, Dalley was confirmed as an Assistant Superintendent of Police (ASP) in 1924.[1]

How did the Malayan Security Service come into existence? The pre-war Inspector General of the Straits Settlements Police, A.H. Dickinson, provided an official account of the genesis of the early MSS and how it was founded when he included it in a list of British pre-war intelligence organizations that he prepared after WWII for Lieutenant General Arthur Earnest Percival, the ill-fated commander of the Allied forces in Malaya and Singapore who surrendered Singapore to the Japanese on 15 February 1942. Percival was then writing his dispatches at the War Office on the Malayan Campaign.[2] Dickinson reported that the MSS was created in September 1939 at the suggestion of MI5, the UK domestic intelligence agency, which then included British overseas colonies within its remit, with the support of the colonial Singapore and Malayan Governments, when it seemed likely that the separate Special Branches in Singapore and Kuala Lumpur would need restructuring and refining to prepare for the possibility of war with Japan. It was established on a pan-Malayan basis as a coordinating and reporting body for political and security intelligence. Its headquarters were at Robinson Road, Singapore, and it had a Malayan branch in Kuala Lumpur, with an MSS officer based in nearly all of the Malayan States and territories. As such, it formed part of what was referred to as the "Singapore Fortress Defence Scheme", which had both military and civil sections. The former were commanded by a "Military Defence Officer" dealing with the armed forces, and the latter by Dickinson, Inspector General of the Straits Settlements Police, who was appointed as "Civil Defence Officer" in charge of police and intelligence matters, with responsibilities stretching from Singapore through Peninsular Malaya up to the northern Malaya/Siam border area, as well as the central control and registration of aliens. The main function of the registration of aliens was to exercise control over the increasing number of

Japanese visitors to Malaya and Singapore, many of whom were Japanese spies operating under cover as businessmen or other innocuous occupations.

Dickinson candidly admitted, however, that by the time of the Japanese invasion, MSS had not yet become fully operational. Although it existed, the sheer rapidity of the Japanese thrust into Malaya heading for Singapore prevented it from becoming as effective as had been intended.

When the British colonial government returned to Singapore after the Japanese surrender in August 1945, the MSS returned with it as the pan-Malayan political intelligence service covering both Singapore and the Malayan Peninsula from its headquarters at Robinson Road, Singapore, adjacent to the Singapore Police Criminal Investigation Department (CID). It was quite separate, however, from the Singapore Police.

A Local Security Officer (LSO) was posted to each of the Malay States except for Kelantan, Terengganu, Melaka, and Pahang, as the MSS did not have sufficient staff to cover all the Malay States, and in these four states arrangements were made for the relevant police CID departments to cover intelligence matters for the MSS. It is not clear why these four territories were selected in this way, but it may well have been that they were not considered to be strongholds of Communist activity.

Be that as it may, it is often overlooked by Dalley's detractors that the MSS, even when it was fully effective (but not at "establishment" strength) in 1948, had only 9 LSOs in Peninsular Malaya and 3 in Singapore, against an approved establishment of 18 and 7, respectively. Dalley was, in fact, so concerned about the situation that he requested the Singapore and Malayan Police Commissioners to provide him with suitable staff to bring the MSS up to strength, but there is no evidence on record that he was able to receive any reinforcements in this way, probably because the police were so absorbed with the investigation of criminal activities that they were unable to do so.[3]

The strength of the senior staff of the MSS and its approved establishment, in its early days on 1 May 1946 when the British returned to Singapore/Malaya after the Japanese surrender, was as follows:

Actual Strength	Approved Establishment
1 Director	1 Director
1 Dy. Director	1 Dy. Director
5 Asst. Directors	5 Asst. Directors
11 Local Security Officers	15 Local Security Officers
42 Asst. Local Security Officers	56 Asst. Local Security Officers
67 Enquiry Staff	81 Enquiry Staff
16 Translators	21 Translators[4]

The imbalance between actual strength and approved establishment is obvious.

The MSS had the following Charter: "A Pan-Malayan Headquarters at present stationed in Singapore will obtain and collate all Security Intelligence emanating from MSS branches throughout the Peninsula and collect and collate information on subversive organisations and personalities in Malaya and Singapore." There was no actual clarification of what action should be taken on intelligence obtained, but perhaps Dalley assumed this would be self-apparent by what he wrote in the following paragraphs:

It is emphasized that MSS should have no executive powers. Actual raids and arrests should be carried out by the regular police acting on advice of MSS, who would thus ensure coordinated action throughout.

(a) Advise the two Governments as to the extent to which Internal Security is threatened by the activities of such organisations.
(b) Maintain a Central Registry of Aliens.
(c) The Defence Security Officers (MI5) would be in close liaison with MSS and be responsible for keeping SIFE (Security Intelligence Far East) [an outpost of MI5] and the Services informed of developments.
(d) MSS would be staffed by: (i) gazetted officers seconded from the Malayan Union Police and Singapore Police (ii) Inspectors and Detectives seconded from the Malayan Union Police and Singapore Police (iii) Office staff, including translators, confidential stenographers, clerks, photographers and telephone operators, appointed directly by MSS at appropriate rates of remuneration having regard to the security class of work they had to handle.
(e) The Regular Police should act on the advice of MSS, for the MSS has no executive powers.
(f) The MSS should co-ordinate action throughout the country; the MSS would obtain and collate all Security Intelligence throughout Malaya. The Defence Security Officers are responsible for keeping SIFE and the Services informed of developments.

The *Malayan Establishment Staff List 1948*[5] (pp. 90–91) provides the following further details of the MSS organization, including the names of its senior officers in 1948, just before it was closed down:

Gazetted Officers, Malayan Security Service 1948

Name	Rank	Location
J.D. Dalley	Director, Pan-Malaya	Singapore
N.G. Morris	Actg. Dy. Director	Singapore
A.E.G. Blades	Asst. Director	Singapore
C.M.J. Kirke	Actg. Dy. Director	Kuala Lumpur
I.S. Wylie	Local Security Officer	Selangor
W. Elphinstone	Local Security Officer	Johor
D.N. Livingstone	Local Security Officer	Kedah/Perlis
H.T.B. Ryves	Local Security Officer	Perak
K.B. Larby	Local Security Officer	Penang
R.W. Quixley	Local Security Officer	Negri Sembilan
J.E. Fairbairn[6]	Local Security Officer	Singapore
R.B. Corridon[7]	Local Security Officer	Singapore
H.J. Woolnough	Local Security Officer	Singapore

Source: *Malayan Establishment Staff List 1948*, pp. 90–91.

The MSS at full strength was a medium-sized organization consisting of 13 British gazetted officers, 44 Asian inspectors, 2 qualified archivists — both of whom were based in Singapore in charge of the MSS Secret Registry — and locally employed clerical and general staff. For a short time in the early post-war period there was a cadre of British inspectors, too.

The clerical and general staff employed at MSS headquarters then was as follows: 8 confidential European lady[8] secretaries; 1 financial assistant; 1 senior (Chinese) interpreter; 11 translators; 2 Japanese translators; 7 clerks and interpreters; 2 stenographers; 2 Malay writers; 1 linotype operator; 1 linotype mechanic; 10 Malay constables; 4 special constables (drivers); 4 peons; 5 general clerical service clerks (including 3 in the Chinese

Section); 4 "locally appointed" security officers (including Major J.E. Fairbairn); 12 assistant local security officers; 34 enquiry staff (including 3 sub-inspectors, 2 staff-sergeants, 5 sergeants and 22 corporals); and 3 motor transport drivers.[9]

The confidential European lady secretaries referred to above, who were cleared to handle classified correspondence, included the wife of Singapore's Chief Secretary, Wilfred Blythe.[10] Vacancies for junior staff such as confidential clerks, stenographers, translators, photographers, drivers and telephone operators were filled by qualified civilians at appropriate rates of remuneration having regard to the nature of their duties.

Dalley was assisted at pan-Malayan headquarters in Singapore by an Acting Deputy Director (Nigel G. Morris), and another Assistant Director (Alan E.G. Blades)[11] was in charge of operations in Singapore. C.M.J. Kirke, the Acting Deputy Director based in Kuala Lumpur, was responsible for MSS operations in Peninsular Malaya.

As will be described in due course, the MSS lasted until it was officially disbanded on the 23 August 1948, not long after the start of the first Malayan Emergency in June 1948, most likely due to the "turf war" which had developed between MSS and MI5, the British domestic intelligence service based in London, which had the ear of the Colonial Office and had opened in 1946 an outpost in Singapore known as SIFE (Security Intelligence Far East). The difference, however, was important, as the MSS was largely a "local" intelligence organization based in Singapore and reporting to the colonial authorities in Singapore and Kuala Lumpur, whereas SIFE reported to MI5 in London, the centre of power of the British Empire, and other more widespread recipients.

Nothing very much is known about Dalley's family life except that his wife Margaret Capel Layard (b. 8 December 1895) had predeceased him. She is briefly mentioned in Mubin Sheppard's *Taman Budiman: Memoirs of an Unorthodox Civil Servant*.[12] It is known, too, that they had two daughters, but unfortunately all efforts to contact them after Dalley's death have been unsuccessful.[13] Dalley's only son, Captain Peter John Layard Dalley, Royal Artillery, who was attached to the British Army Air Corps, was tragically killed in an air crash in February 1958 in Taiping during the Malayan Emergency after Dalley had retired on pension to the UK.[14]

In fact, it is often overlooked by Dalley's detractors that the MSS was seriously handicapped by having only 9 LSOs in Peninsular Malaya and 3 in Singapore against an approved establishment of 18 and 7, respectively, for the two territories, which would have seriously affected its operations.[15] Dalley was, in fact, so concerned at one time about the shortage of qualified staff at his disposal that he approached the Singapore and Malayan Police Commissioners to provide him with suitable staff to bring the MSS up to strength, but there is no evidence on record to show that this was done.[16]

Under this system, how would intelligence obtained by the MSS be distributed? LSOs would provide copies of their intelligence reports to the Chief Police Officers of the states concerned in addition to MSS headquarters at Kuala Lumpur and Singapore. In turn, the Malayan and Singapore MSS headquarters would ensure that the Governors and Commissioners of Police in Malaya and Singapore were kept informed of the situation in their territories, while the overall pan-Malayan Director MSS in Singapore would coordinate information from both territories to prepare what he called his "comic cuts", the *Political Intelligence Journal* (*PIJ*). The MI5 Defence Security Officers (DSOs) in Singapore and Kuala Lumpur for their part would maintain close liaison with the MSS Singapore and Kuala Lumpur headquarters. One of their main functions was to ensure that the Services were kept informed of political and security matters.[17]

While it was reported that some of Dalley's detractors considered him to be "overambitious" and an "Empire builder", these adjectives would appear to be to some extent due to the inter-agency rivalry which soon developed between Dalley/MSS and the British intelligence service/MI5 under Sir Percy Sillitoe in London. As Sillitoe himself, however, was inflexibly determined to establish a branch in Singapore to be known as "SIFE (Security Intelligence Far East)" under Major Winterborn, it would appear the same adjectives that were used for Dalley could just as easily have been applied to Sillitoe.

Notes

1. ASPs were the equivalent of commissioned officers in the British Army.
2. See Report by A.H. Dickinson, CMG, OBE, former Inspector General of Police, Straits Settlements (1939–42) to the Colonial Office dated 12 January 1946, entitled "Organisations in Malaya concerned in the period September 1939–February 1942 with Political Intelligence and Security", BAM Collection, Royal Commonwealth Library, Cambridge University, pp. 1–4.

    In his paper "MI5 and the Cold War in South-East Asia: Examining the Performance of Security Intelligence Far East (SIFE), 1946–1963" Alexander Shaw refers to MSS having been established in 1946, but in actual fact in its earliest form it was established by A.H. Dickinson, Inspector-General, Straits Settlements Police in September 1939.

    In an article in the *Straits Times* (12 January 1946, p. 6), René H. de S. Onraet, who was Dickinson's predecessor as Inspector-General of the Straits Settlements Police (1936–39) and recalled from retirement by the Colonial Office after the Japanese surrender to advise the British Military Administration on the constitution

and re-organization of the Singapore and Malayan Police Special Branches, also adverted to Dickinson forming the MSS in 1939 to amalgamate the work of the Singapore and Malayan Special Branches. See, too, "Second Supplement to the London Gazette of Friday, the 20th of February, 1948", no. 38218, 26 February 1948. Section 1: Pre-War Preparations / Operational Efficiency of Units in Malaya, available at Britain at War <http://www.britain-at-war.org.uk/WW2/London_Gazette/Malaya_and_Netherlands_East_Indies/html/operational_efficiency_of_unit.htm> (accessed 28 October 2002).
3. See Roger Arditti and Philip H.J. Davies, "Rethinking the Rise and Fall", *Journal of Imperial and Commonwealth History* 43, no. 2 (2014): 292–316. See also Dalley's letter dated 13 July 1948, after the Malayan Emergency had started, to the Commissioner-General's Office Singapore: "...the MSS had to attempt to carry out the duties of MSS in spite of being desperately short of staff".
4. See Brian Stewart, *Smashing Terrorism in the Malayan Emergency: The Vital Contribution of the Police* (Kuala Lumpur: Pelanduk, 2004), pp. 329–32, in which Dalley expressed his frustration at the futility of having an organization for the collection of political intelligence if that intelligence was not made use of. He considered that an Inspector General of Police was required for the whole of Malaya "whose primary duty would be Security Intelligence" (p. 331).
5. *Malayan Establishment Staff List 1948* (Singapore: Government Records).
6. J.E. Fairbairn was an LSO appointed directly to the MSS and had not served in the police previously. When the MSS was disbanded in June 1948 he was transferred to the Singapore SB as an acting Cadet Assistant Superintendent of Police after further training.
7. Richard Corridon remained with the Singapore Special Branch for several years after independence before retiring to the UK, and was employed on intelligence assignments allocated to him by Lee Kuan Yew, the first Prime Minister of Singapore (author's notes).
8. The words "European Lady" were part of the job title.
9. See *Malayan Establishment Staff List 1948*.

10. W.L. Blythe (b. 1896) was the author of *The Impact of Chinese Secret Societies in Malaya — A Historical Study* (London: Oxford University Press, 1969). He joined the Malayan Civil Service (MCS) as a cadet in 1921. Unlike most MCS officers, who had an Oxford or Cambridge background, he was a graduate of Liverpool University.
11. Alan E.G. Blades (b. 1907) joined the Singapore Police as a Cadet Assistant Superintendent on 21 February 1930. He was sent to Amoy (Xiamen) in 1932 to study Hokkien, the predominant southern Chinese dialect spoken in Singapore, and in 1939 to Japan to study Japanese. He escaped to India during the Japanese invasion and worked in intelligence in New Delhi from 1942 to 1945. He was a member of the Far Eastern Bureau, Ministry of Information, New Delhi, as Head of the Japanese Unit, Translation and Broadcasting, dealing with long-term and long-range political warfare (see CO 825/38/8). He returned to Singapore after the war and was appointed Director of the Singapore Special Branch on 1 January 1953 and was the last Caucasian Singapore Commissioner of Police, from 19 September 1957 until Singapore's independence. He was the only Caucasian police officer in the Singapore/Malayan police allowed to maintain a neat, closely cropped, white beard, which was probably due to a skin ailment from which he suffered. When the author was in the Johor Special Branch (1949–50), he acted as liaison officer between Johor and the Singapore SB and he used to meet Blades regularly. See "Blades, AEG", in *Who's Who Malaysia 1963*, edited by J. Victor Morais (Kuala Lumpur: Solai, 1964), p. 38.
12. Mubin Sheppard, *Taman Budiman: Memoirs of an Unorthodox Civil Servant* (Kuala Lumpur: Heinemann Educational Books [Asia], 1979).
13. Email to the author from Kenneth Foo dated 29 August 2017. See also Sheppard, *Taman Budiman*.
14. Information provided by Justin Corfield and Michael Thomson. See Cornfield and Thomson, eds., *The Corian 1998* (Corio, Victoria: Geelong Grammar School, 1999), p. 420.

15. Anthony Short, *The Communist Insurrection in Malaya 1948–60* (London: Frederick Muller, 1975). Reprinted as *In Pursuit of Jungle Rats: The Communist Insurrection in Malaya* (Singapore: Cultured Lotus, 2000), p. 34.
16. Arditti and Davies, "Rethinking the Rise and Fall".
17. Dalley handed a complete set of the MSS *PIJ*s for the period 1946–48 to the Bodleian Library. See Stewart, *Smashing Terrorism*, p. 316.

Chapter 2

Lieutenant Colonel John Dalley and Dalforce

Planning for the military administration of Malaya and Singapore after the Japanese Occupation (1942–45) had actually commenced in London from as early as 1943 by the War Office and the Colonial Office. It was during this period that the decision was made to re-establish post-WWII the pan-Malayan Security Service (MSS) that had existed for a brief period before the Japanese invasion of Malaya in December 1941, and the MSS accordingly returned to Singapore with the British Military Administration (BMA) in September 1945 and remained in place when the civil government returned in April 1946.[1]

Immediate Post-war Situation in Singapore

There were difficulties in operating in the troubled and uncertain times that prevailed in Singapore and Malaya in those early days. Singapore was gripped with lawlessness and violence as soon as the Japanese army withdrew to its barracks, and the situation was not helped by the hiatus of several weeks which ensued before the reoccupying British forces landed in Singapore/

Malaya. During this period the Malayan Communist Party (MCP) and its jungle army, the Malayan People's Anti-Japanese Army (MPAJA), Chinese secret societies, and other armed gangs of civilians emerged to take the law into their own hands. It was a virtual "open house" for them in many ways as the rule of the gun prevailed, and first priority had to be given by the returning British colonial forces to restoring public confidence and combating the crime wave by putting police patrols on the streets supported by British troops.[2]

The delay was probably due to some extent to the unexpectedness of the Japanese surrender and the American General Douglas MacArthur in Tokyo requesting Admiral Lord Louis Mountbatten, the British Commander-in-Chief Southeast Asia, based in Kandy, Ceylon, to postpone accepting the surrender of the Japanese forces in Southeast Asia until the Japanese Government and its armed forces, under the authority of the Japanese Emperor, had signed the official surrender documents on the American battleship USS *Missouri* in Tokyo Bay.[3]

Return of the Malayan Security Service (MSS)

When the MSS landed in Singapore with the British Military Administration in 1945, the head of the MSS Singapore Division was Major J.C. Barry, and his counterpart in Kuala Lumpur was Lieutenant Colonel J.M. McLean. Both were pre-war Malayan Special Branch officers. In the *Annual Report of the Singapore Police 1946*, Barry was commended for retrieving many of the pre-war Special Branch records that would otherwise have been lost, which provided a "valuable foundation for the new Central Registry of Records". But both Barry and MacLean were medically unfit following their experiences during the war and they subsequently retired to the UK on medical grounds.

When Barry returned to the UK on sick leave on 26 November 1945, he was replaced by Alan E.G. Blades, a senior pre-war Singapore MSS/SB officer, mentioned in chapter 1. Both Barry and McLean subsequently retired on medical grounds. When G.C. (Guy) Madoc, a senior pre-war Malayan police officer (who was afterwards to become head of the Malayan Special Branch and later Director of Intelligence, Malaya) returned from leave in the UK, he was appointed Deputy Director, MSS, in Kuala Lumpur.[4]

It seems that Dalley had planned ahead to compensate for the deficiencies in the MSS staff after the war by the secondment of Gazetted Police Officers, as well as Inspectors and Detectives from the Singapore and Malayan Police Forces, as mentioned previously. They would be supported by civilian general administrative staff locally appointed. He apparently intended, too, that some Field Security Officers of the British Army's Intelligence Corps should be offered appointments as acting Assistant Superintendents of Police and seconded to the MSS after initial training, but there is no trace in the official records that anything was done about this.

Post-war, Anthony Short, the author of the standard history of the Malayan Communist Party's uprising against the British colonial government in Malaya, *The Communist Insurrection in Malaya 1948–60*,[5] described the MSS as "a sort of super-intelligence organisation" that was "supernumerary to the police and in particular to the CID", and Aslie and Ibrahim in their Malay-language study of the Malayan Police referred to it as the "Malayan Secret Service".[6]

Colonel John Dalley's Early Days and Malay Secret Societies (*Kongsi Gelap*)

Before the outbreak of the Pacific War in 1941, Dalley had served in

Kedah, Selangor, Johor, Perak and Terengganu, which undoubtedly provided him with a wide experience of conventional police duties. However, in 1931, when he was Officer-in-Charge, Police District (OCPD), Kuala Kangsar, he developed a special interest in Malay secret societies (*Kongsi Gelap Melayu*), about which very little at the time had been written, and he was mentioned in Mahani Musa's study of pre-war Malay secret societies in the northern Malay States as having arrested several members of the infamous Bendera Merah Society (Red Flag Society).[7] He was commended, too, in M.L. Wynne's *Triad and Tabut: A Study of the Origin and Diffusion of Chinese and Mohamedan Secret Societies in the Malay Peninsula AD 1800–1935*,[8] a study of the connections between Chinese and Malay secret societies, mainly in north Malaya. On 10 December 1931, for instance, according to Wynne, Dalley addressed a sub-committee of the Perak State Council on this subject, which consisted of the Sultan of Perak (Sultan Iskandar Shah), the British Resident (Bertram Walter Elles), the Raja Muda (Raja Abdul Aziz) and Raja di Hilir (Raja Sir Chulan), with the District Officer, Kuala Kangsar (J.E. Kempe) in attendance, which was quite an unusual honour for a police officer of his rank at the time.

Wynne, then Chief Police Officer, Perak, and Dalley's commanding officer, was subsequently to become Deputy Inspector General of the Straits Settlements Police in Singapore, and in charge of the Singapore Special Branch at the time of the fall of Singapore to the Japanese in February 1942.[9]

Director, CID, Kuala Lumpur

On 1 January 1940, while the war clouds were gathering with Japan, Dalley was promoted as Director of the Criminal Investigation Department (CID), at federal police headquarters in

Kuala Lumpur. The Special Branch of the police in those days was subsumed in the CID and Dalley was able in this appointment to obtain considerable experience of Special Branch work, which was to stand him in good stead when he later became Director of the MSS. It was only several years later that the Special Branch evolved as a separate branch of the police in its own right during the First Malayan Emergency (1948–60) and was no longer a sub-branch of the CID.

Dalley then prepared a secret report entitled "Jungle Ambush Patrols", a copy of which was submitted through the Chief Police Officer, Perak, to the Malayan Commissioner of Police and the Governor and High Commissioner, Sir Shenton Thomas, who discussed it with Lieutenant General A.E. Percival, Commanding Officer, Malaya. Dalley recommended that stay-behind parties should be set up in Malaya in the event of war and the country being overrun by an invading force, to sabotage the invaders' activities, and to provide intelligence about their intentions and movements. However, his plans were rejected by the Governor and Percival on 1 October 1941, just a few months before the Japanese invasion, on the grounds that they would be likely to affect public morale if they were adopted by giving an impression that Malaya would be overrun by Japan in the event of war. Nevertheless, it is interesting to note that earlier in the year, Lieutenant Colonel J.M.L. Gavin, RE, had been allowed to establish in Singapore a small irregular training school for stay-behind parties that was similar in many ways to what Dalley had in mind, but it is likely that Gavin's training school had the support of MI5 in London and Dalley's did not.

Meanwhile, Dalley had already come to the attention of several well-placed and senior public figures in Malaya, such as Norman Cleaveland in Kuala Lumpur, a wealthy, influential American tin-miner and a member of the Malayan Legislative

Council, and Mubin Sheppard (later Tan Sri Haji Dato' Mubin Sheppard), a senior Malayan Civil Service (MCS) officer, who, after independence, retired in Malaya in 1957, converted to Islam, and became a well-known and respected figure in Malaya's cultural life, who wrote prolifically on Malayan history and culture. Both thought highly of Dalley as a police officer.[10]

Tan Chin Tuan, CBE, JP (b. 1908), Chairman of the Overseas-Chinese Banking Corporation and Chairman of several leading agency companies in Singapore, and probably the leading Chinese banker in Malaya at the time, had a high opinion of Dalley, too. Tan was a member of the Singapore Legislative Council and the Singapore Executive Council (1948–55), was Deputy President of the Singapore Chinese Chamber of Commerce, and was elected by the British administration to assist in the post-war reconstruction of Singapore. He eventually became Deputy President of the Singapore Legislative Council.[11]

On one occasion, when Dalley was Chief Police Officer, Johor, Tan requested Dalley's help to deal with a labour problem that had arisen on Tan's Kambau Rubber Estate, Johor, involving the manager who had been "kidnapped" by his employees for the non-payment of their wages and threatened with violence unless they were paid. There was a slump in rubber prices at the time. Tan reported the matter to Dalley, who went out unarmed to the estate accompanied by two Malay police constables, secured the release of the manager, and arrested the ringleader of the labour unrest. According to the law at the time, Chinese who were not British subjects and had been arrested for criminal activities were liable to be banished to China. Shortly afterwards, the wife of the arrested ringleader came to Tan's house in Paya Lebar to appeal for her husband's release. Tan approached Dalley again for help, as he knew that the woman and her family would be destitute if her husband was banished to China.

Dalley was taken aback. "I don't understand. You asked me to arrest the man and now you want me to release him." Tan replied, "I asked the police to arrest him but not to banish him."

Dalley relented and released the man on Tan providing a surety of a thousand dollars for the man's good behaviour. Afterwards the man and his family came to visit Tan and in Chinese style bowed to thank him for his help. Subsequently, he helped Tan Chin Tuan on many occasions to settle labour problems on rubber estates, where many of the rubber tappers had fallen on bad times during the Great Depression, and he became virtually Tan's unofficial bodyguard until they lost touch with each other during the Japanese Occupation.[12]

Dalforce

When the Japanese invaded Malaya in December 1941, Dalley soon became well-known as the commander of "Dalforce", a guerrilla unit named after him that played a significant part in the defence of Singapore. In the last week of December 1941, a few days before the Japanese invasion, the Singapore Governor Sir Shenton Thomas convened a meeting of leading Chinese to urge them to lend their support to the government in defending Malaya, and an Overseas Chinese Mobilisation Committee headed by Tan Kah Kee, a prominent Chinese community leader, was formed to recruit Chinese members for this purpose.

The British attitude towards the various Chinese groups — in particular, the Malayan Communist Party, which they had banned before the war — took a different turn after the Japanese invaded Malaya on 8 December 1941, and cooperation from the local people, including the communists, was regarded as crucial in repelling the Japanese invasion. The Secretary of State for the Colonies, in a confidential telegram to the Governor, explained:

> In present situation particular importance must be attached to fullest use being made of services of Chinese community in Malaya to defeat the Japanese invasion ... post-war repercussions do not concern us in this emergency. The toughest elements which have given us so much trouble in the past ... are likely to be amongst the most useful for the immediate purposes. I appreciate that this change of attitude may present difficulties for your officers in many directions and particularly to Secretary for Chinese Affairs, whose duties hitherto must necessarily have brought him and his Department into conflict with those elements.[13]

As a result of the help provided by Tan Kah Kee, a large force of Chinese guerrillas, totalling around two thousand, was formed by Dalley in Kuala Lumpur from a motley group of Chinese — some of whom had been detained by the British pre-war for Communist activities and released from prison to serve with Dalforce — which was augmented by Chinese students, school teachers, rickshaw pullers and labourers. They were divided into companies, each under the command of a British officer. Dalley's second-in-command was Major Foh Toh Cheng. Dalley, who was then a Superintendent in the Malayan Police Special Branch, was granted a war-time commission as a Lieutenant Colonel in the British Army's General List.[14]

Although the MCP had been banned pre-war and many known Communists detained, the Singapore Governor agreed in this instance to release Communists from prison, and the ban on the MCP was rescinded. An official account of what happened is provided in the MSS *Political Intelligence Journal* no. 11/48 dated 15 June 1948, quoted here:

> The Chinese Section of the Singapore Special Branch put out feelers on 16 December 1941 for the formation of a united organisation to mobilise Chinese activities to resist the effects

of bombing and profit from the lessons of Penang. A surprising unanimous result followed. The Kuomintang, the China Relief Fund group, the Chinese Chamber of Commerce and the Communists, all came to the Special Branch with what amounted to demands that a Mobilisation Organisation should be set up, and that party and clique differences should be sunk in a common purpose. All parties however — and this point is most significant — insisted that Tan Kah Kee was the only person who could successfully command the support of the broad masses of the Chinese population in the fulfilment of the project.

Mr. Tan Kah Kee, who had already made arrangements to leave the country, was most reluctant to accept leadership, and it looked for a time as if it would fail, but after strenuous efforts between the 18 and 24 December by the Chinese Section of the Special Branch, supplemented by the Chinese Consul General [Kuomintang], Mr. Kao Ling Pai, Mr. George K.C. Yeh, representative of the China International Publicity Bureau, and Mr. Wing Choo, the President of the Chinese Chamber of Commerce, Mr. Tan Kah Kee was persuaded to accept the leadership of a 'Mobilisation Council' for Singapore, on which all shades of Chinese opinion agreed to serve.

The Council compromised 95 members as follows:

- All dialects and Guilds — 31 seats
- Kuomintang — 10 seats
- Malayan Communist Party — 10 seats
- Straits-born Chinese — 10 seats
- Chinese women — 4 seats
- Culturists, newspapers, etc. — 10 seats
- Labour organizations — 10 seats
- Unallocated — 10 seats

The first party of Communist guerrillas were trained in Singapore in December 1941 under arrangements made by the

Special Branch. But it was a case of a race against time. When Dalforce during the course of fighting withdrew to Singapore, it was augmented by Chinese volunteers.[15] Although Dalforce was not fully trained or equipped and was armed in many cases with shotguns or hunting rifles, each with a limited supply of bullets, some hand grenades, and spears rather than modern weapons, it earned a reputation for fighting bravely alongside the Australian Army against the invading Japanese during the Malayan campaign. It had a company attached to the Australian 2/20 Battalion, which was part of the 3rd Indian Corps. In its final days in Singapore, Dalforce had a total of five companies or units, each of about a hundred troops, deployed at the following locations:

- 1 Company at Jurong (18th milestone)
- 1 Company attached to the Australian 2/20 Battalion at Sarimbun Beach
- 1 Company in the area between Serangoon River and Pasir Ris (sometimes referred to as the "Company at Hougang")
- 1 Company in the Johor-Singapore Causeway sector
- 1 Overseas Chinese Guard Platoon stationed at Kranji.

The Singapore HQ and training School for Dalforce was established by Tan Kah Kee in 1941 at the Nanyang Normal School on Kim Yam Road, Singapore. After WWII, the campus was used by a newly established Chinese secondary school, the Nan Chiau Girls' High School, until finally, in 2001, the school relocated to Seng Kang New Town.

Since they were not issued with military uniforms, Dalforce fighters wore civilian clothes, with white canvas shoes, yellow "bandanas" around their heads and a triangular piece of red cloth on their right arms. A film in which this "uniform" is worn was shown at the time.[16]

Most of the men were armed with WWI Lee Enfield (.303) rifles, each issued with twenty-four rounds of ammunition and bayonets. Others were provided with single- or double-barrelled shotguns used for hunting wild animals, and long-bladed Malay *parangs* (knives). A few hand grenades were also distributed. There was only time to provide about ten days' military training before they were thrown into action against the Japanese.

There was perhaps a general feeling among Dalforce that the British were being unfair to them, because they saw that British, Australian and Indian soldiers were better equipped than they were, although they did not realize that several tons of arms and ammunition destined for them went down with the troopship *Empress of Asia*, which was sunk approaching Singapore on 5 February 1942 by Japanese dive-bombers.[17]

Dalforce distinguished itself in several bitter battles after the Japanese invading force crossed the Straits of Johor into Singapore, especially near Bukit Timah as the Japanese advanced towards the centre of Singapore, and Dalforce fought hand-to-hand against the Japanese in Bukit Timah, Woodlands, Kranji and at Sarimbun on the west coast. Of the troops that defended Singapore, Dalforce was said to be among the most motivated to fight the Japanese.[18]

On 13 February 1942, two days before the surrender of Singapore, Lieutenant Colonel Dalley demobilized Dalforce and paid the members a demobilization allowance. It is reported that several escaped to Sumatra and from there managed to get back to India to join the British forces there, and others went into the Malayan jungle and joined the MCP's Malayan People's Anti-Japanese Army (MPAJA), which was supported by British officers of the clandestine British Force 136.

Dalley added another untold dimension to the Dalforce story when he related after his retirement to an old friend, Hugh Bryson, a former senior MCS officer, then editor of the journal of the British Association of Malaya (BAM) in London, that in 1941 when he commanded Dalforce, the Hung League Chinese secret society members (Kuomintang) would not fight alongside the Han Chinese secret society members (MCP), and the impasse had to be resolved by forming separate companies. Later, during the Japanese Occupation, the Han group set up their headquarters in the Malayan jungle in the area extending from Kuala Kangsar to Grik, while the area controlled by the Hung group occupied the area from Sungei Siput and included most of Johor. These areas had always been traditionally Han and Hung areas.[19]

Escape from Singapore

Dalley's last few days in Singapore were most dramatic. Captain G.F.A. Mulock, RN, one of the last remaining senior Royal Navy officers in Singapore, was ordered to report for further orders to the office of Lieutenant General Percival, GOC, Singapore, at Fort Canning at 2200 hours on the evening of 14 February, a day before the British surrender. Mulock was informed that the Governor and Percival had decided that some forty senior Special Branch and MSS officers, MCS officers and some key Australian diplomats based in Singapore should be evacuated that evening, and he was ordered to requisition the motor launches *Osprey* and *Mary Rose* for this purpose.[20]

On arrival at the quayside, Mulock's group was confronted by a group of Australian Army deserters armed with Thomson submachine guns and hand grenades. The members of Mulock's group were able, however, to make their way to the *Osprey*, although the deserters opened fire and machine-gunned the launch. Fortunately, there were no casualties and, after an attempt by the deserters to board the launch was thwarted, some thirty-eight individuals were ferried out to the *Mary Rose,* a 40-foot (12m) motor launch, at 2330 hours on 14 February 1942.

Captain Mulock took with him six Malay seamen from HMS *Sultan*. Among the launch's thirty-eight passengers were Lieutenant Colonel Dalley of Dalforce and five of his officers; H.B. Sym, Head of the Malayan SB; Lieutenant Colonel H.L. Hill, OBE, 4/19th Hyderabad Regiment, Indian Army; Major K.S. Morgan, Head of the Japanese Section of the Singapore SB; M.L. Wynne, then Deputy Inspector General of the Straits Settlements Police; Vivian Gordon Bowden, Australian Trade Commissioner in Singapore; A.N. Wootton, Commercial Secretary, Australian Trade Commission, Singapore; and Captain Charles Corry (MCS).

On the evening of 16 February 1942, the *Mary Rose* was well on its way to Bangka when it was illuminated by searchlights from two Japanese patrol vessels in the Muntok Straits behind the Moesi River, which threatened to open fire on the launch. Captain Mulock refused to surrender, but a close warning shot across the bows forced him to do so. An English-speaking Japanese officer came aboard the launch and Captain Mulock surrendered to him.

The launch was escorted to Muntok Harbour, Bangka Island, where its occupants were taken ashore as prisoners of war. Captain Mulock and the six Malay sailors remained aboard until the Imperial Japanese Navy came for them. The prisoners were held in a cinema hall at Muntok. When the Australian Commissioner V.G. Bowden told his captors in Japanese — he had formerly been stationed in Japan and spoke some Japanese — of his diplomatic status and remonstrated with some Japanese soldiers who attempted to remove his personal possessions, he was punched, taken outside the cinema hall, and shot dead.[21]

Dalley became a prisoner of war of the Japanese at Muntok, where he remained from 17 February 1942 to 7 March 1942.

According to a record that Dalley provided at the end of the war (see photoplates), he went through the wire at night from Muntok on 7 March 1942 and travelled by sea to Java where he was recaptured by the Japanese on 24 April 1942. Fortunately for him, they did not realize he had escaped from Muntok.[22] He claimed, too, that he made several attempts to escape from Japanese custody in Java, and although he was not detected by the Japanese, he was not successful in escaping either.

Dalley spent most of his time as a POW in a Japanese POW camp in Mukden, Manchuria, cut off from the war. He did not have much to say after the war about his stay there, as he was completely cut off from the news. It is not clear whether this was the same camp where General Percival was detained; it appears that it was the policy of the Japanese to move senior officers of the rank of colonel and above to Japan and Manchuria to separate them from the rank and file of the POWs.[23]

Dalley's path to Manchuria led through a number of countries, which are listed in the document related to his capture (reproduced in the photoplates), where Dalley spent relatively short periods, such as Tanjong Priok, May 1942 – September 1943; Changi, September–October 1943; Shirakawa, Taiwan, November 1943 – February 1945; Mita, Japan, March–April 1945; and thence, via Korea, to Mukden in Manchuria, where at the end of the war, after Russia declared war on Japan, he was released by the advancing Russian Army.

It seems likely, nevertheless, that he must have been giving thought to his future in MSS as, while he was on recuperative leave in England before he returned to Singapore, he wrote to Sir Edward Gent, the British High Commissioner in Malaya, and Malcolm MacDonald, the British Commissioner-General for Southeast Asia, and perhaps other senior British colonial officials in Singapore, about the plans he had for what seems to be MSS.[24]

In April 1946, for instance, he wrote from his address at Marstin House, Marstin Magna, near Yeovil, Somerset, to Sir Edward Gent with his suggestions for establishing a "Political Intelligence Bureau in Malaya" and provided an outline of "political intelligence duties and the number of branches required" for it. Unfortunately, a copy of this letter does not appear to have survived, but Gent replied that he would see how far the Colonial Office had digested his (Dalley's) suggestions and that he would get back to him. Malcolm MacDonald, who was then temporarily staying at The Residency, Penang, before he moved to Bukit Serene, Johor Baru, must have received a copy of the letter, too, as he acknowledged receipt on 10 July 1946.

On 23 July 1946, Dalley wrote again from Yeovil referring to the malevolent influence of Malay political societies in Malaya in which he had always been interested, such as, for example, Kesatuan Melayu Muda (KMM), which had been recognized by the Japanese during their occupation of Malaya, and was a Malayan counterpart of the Indonesian Puteri Permuda Indonesia.

It is interesting that the Secretary of State for the Colonies wrote to Dalley on 28 July 1946 that the views of the Inspector-General of the Palestine Police, Lieutenant Colonel W.N.(Nicol) Gray had been sought about Dalley's suggestions concerning what he called a "Political Intelligence Bureau" in Malaya, which sounded very much like the MSS which had been formed in 1939. He informed Dalley that in Gray's view the MSS should be absorbed into the Federation of Malaya Police, "otherwise there may be a continued detriment to efficiency [sic]" as the "Commissioner of Police must be in sole control of the police force". There is no indication on the file of Dalley's reply.

The British Palestine Police was then in the process of being disbanded, and as H.B. Langworthy, a senior pre-war Malayan Police officer, who was then the Commissioner of Police, Malaya, was returning to the UK for medical treatment, the Colonial Office took the opportunity to instruct Colonel Gray to visit Malaya to report on the post-war state of the Malayan Police. Gray's subsequent report indicated that police morale was low, its equipment outdated, and the entire force needed retraining following the Japanese Occupation.

Meanwhile, C.W.D. Hall, the Deputy Commissioner of Police, asked Gray why no action had been taken by the UK to supply the indents he had submitted for police wireless sets, automatic weapons, and transport, but Sydney Palmer, an unofficial member of the Malayan Executive Council and a prominent member of the Finance Committee who was involved, replied, "You can't blame the Finance Committee: we were never asked to find the funds."

When Gray returned to London to present his report, it was decided that as Langworthy was retiring on medical grounds, and the Palestine Police was being wound up, Gray should be offered the appointment of Commissioner of Police, Malaya. In accepting the appointment, Gray laid down several conditions for doing so, which included the employment of a number of officers who had served under him in the Palestine Police, as well as the provision of an aircraft to be placed at his disposal as Commissioner of Police. Although he did not get an aircraft, a large number of hand-picked former members of the Palestine Police were appointed to the Malayan Police, the first batch of which accompanied Gray when he flew out to Kuala Lumpur on 12 August 1948 to take up his appointment. In some cases, as the former Palestine officers held higher ranks than Malayan police officers of longer service, the arrangements did not do much to improve the morale of the Malayan police. However, after some time the situation settled down and the forty or so former Palestine Police officers that Gray had brought out with him, as well as others who joined them later, helped considerably to restore the morale by example and intensive training. It was just in time, too, as the first Malayan Emergency (1948–60), the Malayan Communist Party's uprising to overthrow the British colonial government and establish a Communist People's Republic of Malaya in its place, had started in June 1948.[25]

To return to Dalley, he can be considered to have been fortunate in one way. Although he was captured by the Japanese after he escaped from Singapore and spent the war years in inaccessible Mukden in Manchuria, he was probably one of the few senior Singapore/Malayan Police officers with an SB/MSS intelligence background and an impressive knowledge of Malay politics to have survived the war. Most of the senior Singapore/Malayan MSS/SB officers had been killed in the war or were medically unfit for further service as a result of the ill treatment they had received from the Japanese as POWs. The brilliant M.L. Wynne, author of *Triad and Tabut*; H.B. Sym, the pre-war head of the Malayan Special Branch; and D. Mathieson, another experienced Malayan intelligence officer, died in Sumatra after their escape from Singapore. Major K.S. Morgan, the head of the Japanese Section of the Singapore SB, a former regular Indian Army officer who was a qualified Indian Army first-class interpreter in Japanese and Russian and who at one time had been on the British-Indian Army Intelligence Staff in Simla and had been head-hunted to join the Singapore SB, survived the war but his health had suffered as a POW and he retired on medical grounds.

Notes

1. *Annual Report of the Singapore Police Force 1946* (Singapore: Singapore Government Printer, 1947). The Japanese surrendered on 15 August 1945.

2. Ibid.
3. Leon Comber, *Singapore Chronicles: Japanese Occupation* (Singapore: Institute of Policy Studies, National University of Singapore/Straits Times Press, 2017), pp. 70–72.
4. Letters to author dated 10 June 1994 and 10 March 1995 from G.(Guy) C. Madoc, CBE, KPM, CPM. Madoc is an interesting person. He joined the Federated Malay States as a police cadet in 1920. He was captured at the fall of Singapore and became a POW at Changi. During his incarceration, he studied Thai. He was promoted to Superintendent of Police in 1948 and posted undercover as First Secretary (Malayan Affairs) in the British Embassy, Bangkok. On returning to Kuala Lumpur, he was promoted to Assistant Commissioner of Police (ACP) and in 1952 he became head of the Federal Special Branch with the rank of Senior Assistant Commissioner of Police (SAC 'E'). In 1954 he was promoted to Director of Intelligence, Malaya. With the abolition of the post of Director of Intelligence upon Malayan independence in 1957, he became Deputy Secretary (Security and Intelligence), Defence Department. He retired to the Isle of Man in 1959, where he was a Member of the Police Authority of the Isle of Man (1963–88). Undated letter (probably March 1995) from Madoc to author. See also *Colonial Office List* (London: HM Stationery Office, 1957).
5. Anthony Short, *The Communist Insurrection in Malaya, 1948–60* (London: Frederick Muller, 1975). Reprinted as *In Pursuit of Jungle Rats: The Communist Insurrection in Malaya* (Singapore: Cultured Lotus, 2000).
6. See Short, *The Communist Insurrection*; and Mohd Reduan Haji Aslie and Mohd Radzuan Haji Ibrahim, *Polis di- Raja Malaysia: Sejarah, Peranan dan Cabaran* [The Royal Malaysian Police: History, role and challenge] (Kuala Lumpur: Kumpulan Karangraf, 1987), p. 311.
7. See Mahani Musa, *Kongsi Gelap Melayu di Negri-Negri Utara Pantai Barat Semenanjung Tanah Melayu 1821–1940-an* [Malay secret societies in the Northern Malay States 1821–1940s], JMBRAS Monograph no. 36 (Kuala Lumpur: JMBRAS, 2012).

8. M.L. Wynne, *Triad and Tabut: A Study of the Origin and Diffusion of Chinese and Mohamedan Secret Societies in the Malay Peninsula, AD 1800–1935* (Singapore: Government Printing Office, 1941).
9. The author is grateful to Kenneth Foo for providing information about Wynne, who escaped from Singapore at the time of the British surrender with several other senior British officers. He was captured by the Japanese in Sumatra, who fortunately did not realize the position he had held in Malaya, and later died of illness in Pladjoe, Sumatra, on 4 April 1942. His ashes were later laid to rest in April 1948 in the Bidadari Cemetery, Singapore, and subsequently transferred to the Kranji War Cemetery, Singapore, where a tombstone was erected over his grave.

    A limited edition of Wynne's book referred to earlier was printed for internal distribution by the Singapore Government Printer in 1941, but most of this edition seems to have disappeared during the Japanese Occupation. It was, however, reprinted post-war in a limited edition for internal distribution by the Singapore Government, and although it has now become rare, a copy of the original edition is available in the Singapore National Library for consultation by appointment only.
10. See Norman Cleaveland, *Bang! Bang! in Ampang: Dredging Tin in Malaya's Emergency* (San Pedro: Symecon, 1973), pp. 81–82; and Mubin Sheppard, *Taman Budiman*, pp. 34–35.

    Norman Cleaveland (b. 1901), Stanford University, was a very colourful person: an Olympic Games Gold Medallist in Paris for Rugby Football (1924), a pilot in the US Air Force during WWII (1942–45), a member of the US Reparation Commission for Korea and Manchuria (1946), member of the Malayan War Damage Commission (1948–56), member of the Selangor War Executive Council (1953), manager of Pacific Tin Consolidated Corporation (1948–50) and president since 1950. See J. Victor Morais, ed., *Who's Who Malaysia 1963* (Kuala Lumpur: Solai, 1964), p. 61.

    Mubin Sheppard (1905–94), PPT, CMG, MBE, JP, subsequently Tan Sri Haji Dato Dr Mubin Sheppard, was educated at Marlborough, a top British public school, read history at Cambridge, and was appointed as a Cadet Administrative Officer in the Malayan Civil Service (MCS) in 1928. He filled many senior appointments in the MCS. He became a POW of the Japanese during WWII, but post-war he held several senior appointments in the Malayan Civil Service, such as British Advisor, Kelantan (1950–51), British Advisor, Negri Sembilan (1951–56), Head Malayan Emergency Food Denial Organisation (1956–57), and Keeper of the Rulers' Seal and Malayan Public Records. On retiring from the MCS, he converted to Islam, adopted the name Mubin Sheppard and decided to remain in Malaya. He wrote prolifically about Malayan culture and history, including the authorized biography of Tunku Abdul Rahman, the first Prime Minister of Malaya. See Morais, *Who's Who Malaysia 1963*, p. 235.

11. See Lee Su Yin, *Rock Solid: The Corporate Career of Tan Chin Tuan* (Singapore: Landmark Books, 2006), pp. 91–92. See also "Tan Chin Tuan", in *MSS Who's Who*, serial no. 5, P.F. 1/39, Secret, and Morais, *Who's Who Malaysia 1963*, p. 256.

12. Lee, *Rock Solid*, p. 94.

13. Lee Su Yin, *British Policy and the Chinese in Singapore, 1939 to 1955: The Public Service Career of Tan Chin Tuan* (Singapore: Talisman, 2011), p. 45.

14. See *Supplement 4343 to the London Gazette*, 1946, HM Stationery Office, issue no. 3774, Lieutenant Colonel John Dalley (359922).

15. *British Military Administration (Malaya) Papers*, 1945–46, MLF11; MLF377, HQ Chief Civil Affairs Officer, British Military Administration of Malaya (BMA), Kuala Lumpur, 8 January 1946; and Peter Elphick, *Far Eastern File: The Intelligence War in the Far East, 1930–1945* (London: Hodder and Stoughton, 1997), p. 338.

16. "Location Scouting in British Newsreels Made before the Japanese Occupation of Singapore (1938–42)", *The Hunter: Location Scouting in Singapore's Filmic History* (blog) <https://sgfilmhunter.wordpress.com/tag/newsreel/> (accessed 16 October 2017). "Dalforce" was featured, too, in the Singapore Broadcasting Corporation's 1984 television series *The Awakening* and in MediaCorp's 2001 drama *A War Diary*.

17. Ralph Modder, *The Passionate Islanders — Singapore at War, 1941–42* (Singapore: Horizon Books, 2010), pp. 208–9.
18. Kevin Blackburn and Chew Ju Ern Daniel, "Dalforce at the Fall of Singapore in 1941: An Overseas Chinese Heroic Legend", *Journal of Chinese Overseas* 1, no. 2 (2005): 242–43; Daniel Chew Ju Ern, "Reassessing the Overseas Chinese Legend of Dalforce at the Fall of Singapore", academic exercise for BA (Hons.) History, NIE, Nanyang Technological University, Singapore, 2005; and Malcolm M. Murfett, John N. Miksic, Brian P. Farrell, and Chiang Ming Shun, *Between Two Oceans: A Military History of Singapore from 1275 to 1971*, 2nd ed. (Singapore: Marshall Cavendish International [Asia], 2011), p. 227.
19. *British Association of Malaya Historical Collection*, BAM II/49 (NAB 465) "Secret Societies & Guerrilla Bands in 1947", Correspondence from J.D. Dalley 1947–1965.
20. See Darryl Bennet, "Bowden, Vivian Gordon (1884–1942)", *Australian Dictionary of Biography*, vol. 13 (Canberra: National Centre of Biography, Australian National University, 1993) <http://adb.anu.edu.au/biography/bowden-vivian-gordon-9552> (accessed 29 January 2017).
21. See Robert Hughes-Mullock, FRAS, "White Ribbon, White Flag: The Life and Times of Captain G.F.A. Mulock, DSO, RN", *Review Journal of the Naval Historical Collectors and Research Association* 19, no. 2 (2006).
22. Confidential, "M.I.9/Jap, No. 49254A, Lieutenant Colonel John Douglas Dalley", a copy of which was supplied to the author by Kenneth Foo on 25 March 2015. Dalley reported that Lieutenant A.E. Eno, General List (attached to Dalforce in Malaya), Leading Seaman T. Parson, and Sergeant K. Wharton, AIF, accompanied him on his escape from Muntok, Bangka, but they were recaptured on 24 April 1942. He was not aware of what happened to them afterwards.
23. Lieutenant-General A.E. Percival, *The War in Malaya* (New Delhi: Sagar, 1971), p. 321; and Kevin Y.L. Tan, *Marshall of Singapore: A Biography* (Singapore: Institute of Southeast Asian Studies, 2008), p. 122.

24. "Malcolm MacDonald Papers", box 16, Durham University Library, MAC 15/02/1-58, file 2 of 2, S.E. Asia, Governor-General: Colonel Dalley 1946–1948, microfilm no. NAB 1534.
25. *British Association of Malaya (BAM) Historical Collection*, Political & Constitutional, BAM1/24, "The Malayan Police". Lieutenant Colonel W.N.(Nicol) Gray, DSO and bar, CMG, KPM, a wartime Lieutenant Colonel in the Royal Marines, had a distinguished war record and served as Commissioner of Police, Malaya, for several years until he resigned in January 1952 after a disagreement with Sir William Jenkin, Director of Intelligence, over the role of the Malayan Police Special Branch.

Chapter 3

The Establishment of "Security Intelligence Far East (SIFE)" in Singapore

Before Dalley returned to Singapore from the UK in February 1947, considerable consternation was caused in Singapore by the receipt of a rather extraordinary telegram dated 2 September 1946 from the Colonial Office addressed to Malcolm MacDonald, then Governor-General for Southeast Asia, with copies to the local Singapore and Kuala Lumpur Governors. Seemingly without any further introduction, it forwarded a proposal by Sir Percy Sillitoe, Head of MI5, the UK domestic intelligence organization, whose remit extended to British colonies, to establish a branch to be known as "Security Intelligence Far East (SIFE)" in Singapore.[1]

Colonial Office Telegram to Malcolm MacDonald

It arrived literally out of the blue, as there had not been any prior notice of Sillitoe's proposal and, indeed, there is nothing in the records to indicate that the matter had been under consideration, although clearly it must have been discussed in the Colonial Office. It included an attachment dated 6 August 1946, some weeks before the date of the actual telegram, which was headed "Memorandum of Instruction", covering the appointment of Lieutenant Colonel C.E. Dixon as Head of SIFE, as well as a "Charter" for SIFE indicating its proposed functions.

As the telegram explained:

> The documents were, of course, first submitted in draft for approval here [presumably by MI5 to the Colonial Office], but as the Security Service [MI5] were most anxious to secure general approval with their provisions without delay, and in view of the fact that the relations of SIFE with Colonial Governments will generally be through Defence Security Officers whose duties are defined in a standard form of their own Memorandum of Instructions, it was in the circumstances agreed that general approval could be given without submitting the drafts to the Governors for comment.[2]

This certainly seemed to be, to say the least, a rather unusual method on the part of the Colonial Office to issue "instructions" to Singapore/Malaya, especially as Dalley had been available for consultation in the UK and the MSS in Singapore would be affected. As could be expected, the telegram caused some consternation in Singapore and the matter was considered at some length at several high-level meetings.

The initial reaction of L.F. Knight, the acting Director of MSS before Dalley returned to Singapore, was understandably "fairly strong", and he suggested to the Singapore Commissioner of Police that the matter should be discussed as soon as possible by the Commissioner, Colonel Dixon, who was already in Singapore, and himself. He felt that a "normal" reading of the telegram could only mean that a rival organization to MSS was about to be established in Singapore, which would inevitably lead to MSS's redundancy. Although Knight commented to the Singapore Commissioner of Police that his reactions had been modified somewhat by Colonel Dixon, whom he had met, providing him with a better understanding of the situation, nevertheless, he still considered that the functions of MSS and SIFE would overlap to some extent if both operated in Singapore, especially as it was intended that while MSS would remain the Governor's advisor for "all matters of Malayan security interest", SIFE at the same time would be allowed to advise the Governor on the "broader aspects of intelligence". He saw little difference between the two functions. Moreover, as Knight pointed out, SIFE would not run its own agents in Singapore/Malaya and it would have to obtain intelligence from MSS/SB, which carried out this function.

He thought it quite likely, too, that MI5 would "arrange" in due course for SIFE to be located at Phoenix Park when the headquarters of Malcolm MacDonald, the British Governor General for Southeast Asia, were moved there, which would be likely to give the impression that SIFE was senior to MSS.

It is clear, too, from the minutes of a high-level Governor's Conference held at Penang at the time to discuss the CO's telegram, that there was considerable widespread "unease" about the "SIFE Charter" and the unorthodox way Sillitoe's proposals had apparently been accepted by the Colonial Office without seeking the views in the first place of Malcolm MacDonald and the Governors of Singapore and Malaya on how MI5's proposals would be likely to affect MSS.

It may therefore perhaps be appropriate at this stage to examine the SIFE Charter, dated 6 August 1946, which was attached to the telegram sent by the Colonial Office to MacDonald, and compare it with the more mundane MSS Charter.

The SIFE Charter

The "SIFE Charter" undoubtedly had a more "professional" look about it than its more humble MSS equivalent. Overall, in a political sense, it virtually provided a mandate for running British intelligence operations, not only in Singapore/Malaya but also in other British territories in the area, which would be more in keeping with MI5's overall mandate, as opposed to MSS's more local concern, which was limited to Singapore/Malaya. It reported, as expected, in the first place to MI5, its parent organization in London, and then beyond to local Defence Committees and local Commanders-in-Chief. It stressed, too, the importance of maintaining close relations with MI6, the British foreign intelligence service, which in some ways was rather unusual, as MI5 had traditionally not worked closely with MI6. SIFE, therefore, was not entirely a branch of MI5 but it was used as a base as well for some MI6 officers covering non-British territories in the Far East.

The text of the SIFE Charter reads as follows:

SIFE is an inter-Services organisation responsible for the collection and dissemination of all security intelligence affecting British territories in the Far East to interested and appropriate Service and Civil Departments.

(a) Head/SIFE is responsible to the Director General of the Security Service [Sir Percy Sillitoe] and locally in Singapore to the Defence Committee jointly and the Commanders-in-Chief individually. His responsibilities to the authorities in Burma will be determined when their position has been clarified.

(b) Head/SIFE is the 'theatre head' for the Security Services and in this capacity responsible for ensuring that the flow of intelligence to and from the Defence Security Officers [DSOs] in the Far East meets the requirements of SIFE. He will also be responsible for the distribution of SIFE staff throughout the theatre in accordance with current requirements.

(c) Head/SIFE will be a member of the Joint Intelligence Committee, Singapore, as the SIFE representative in Hong Kong will be a member of the Joint Intelligence Committee, Hong Kong.

(d) SIFE will maintain close relations with MI6 in the Far East. It will maintain liaison for the same purpose with the Director, Intelligence Bureau, Government of India, and the Director of the Australian Commonwealth Security Service, and other Security Service links overseas.

(e) SIFE cannot be called upon to reveal its sources of information to any other organisation or outside authority. It is, however, within the discretion of Head/SIFE to do so in a case where he considers it desirable or expedient to do so, subject to obtaining the consent of any other organisation which may control or have an interest in the matter. In important cases, the matter should be referred to the Director General of the Security Service [MI5].

During the period 1946 to 1963, the Heads/SIFE were changed fairly frequently. For the record, they were: Lieutenant Colonel C.E. Dixon (1946); Malcolm Johnson (1946–47); Hugh Winterborn (1947–48); Alex Kellar (1948–49); Jack Morton (1949–52);[3] Dr Courtney Young (1952–53); Richard Thistlewaite (1955–59); Michael F. Serpell (1960–62); and Christopher Albert Herbert (1962–63).[4]

The MSS Charter

As to be expected, in contrast to SIFE's wider and more ambitious approach, the MSS Charter was effectively limited geographically to the general area of Singapore and Malaya, and was considerably more "local" in its approach, although its fortnightly *Political Intelligence Journal* (*PIJ*) had a wide circulation.

The main functions of MSS, which Dalley sent to Sir Ralph Hone in the Commissioner-General's Office, Singapore, as at August 1948, were as follows:[5]

(a) To collect and collate information on subversive and political organisations and personalities in Malaya and Singapore.
(b) To advise the two Governments [Singapore and Malaya] as to the extent in which internal security is threatened by the activities of such organisations.
(c) To keep the two Governments informed of the trends of public opinion which affect, or are likely to affect, the security of Singapore/Malaya.
(d) To maintain a Central Registry of Aliens.
(e) To maintain close liaison with other friendly security intelligence organisations and with the D.S.O.s.
(f) To exercise supervision of the Mecca Pilgrimage.

The "supervision" of the Mecca Pilgrimage refers to the duties of a Malay officer assigned to escort pilgrims to Mecca who was then required on his return to Singapore to prepare a report for the MSS on any "anti-British" propaganda or lectures the pilgrims were exposed to in Mecca by the Saudi Arabian authorities.

It should perhaps be noted, too, that a decision was made in London in early 1943 by the Colonial Office and the War Office in planning for the re-occupation of Singapore/Malaya at the end of the Pacific War that the MSS would be appointed as "the sole political and security intelligence agency for Singapore/Malaya" and that it would accompany the British Military Administration of Malaya (BMA) to Singapore. This decision therefore seemed to precede by a few years Sillitoe's proposal to set up a branch of MI5 in Singapore.[6]

Moreover, it should not be overlooked that an earlier form of MSS had actually been established in Singapore in September

1939, as adverted to previously, by A.H. Dickinson, the pre-war Inspector-General of the Straits Settlements Police, Singapore, which he included in the report he prepared for General Percival when the latter was writing his dispatches after the war on the fall of Singapore.[7] According to Dickinson's account, MSS was established *at the suggestion of MI5* (author's italics), with the concurrence of the Governors of Singapore and Malaya, and it would therefore be rather surprising if Sillitoe was not aware of this when he sent his proposal to establish SIFE in Singapore in September 1946.

During the many discussions that were held in Singapore, the Singapore Colonial Secretary remarked that it would "seem essential that if SIFE were to be established in Singapore there should be harmony between the two intelligence agencies", and it was therefore agreed to appoint what was referred to as a "final" sub-committee of Dixon (proposed Head/SIFE) and L.F. Knight (Acting Head/MSS) to discuss the matter further and make recommendations to MacDonald and the two Governors on how the matter should be settled.

Even so, in spite of this last-minute effort, differences persisted. It would seem, though, that in the end the view of the Colonial Office in London prevailed. As Christopher Andrew, the eminent historian of British intelligence, comments in his *The Defence of the Realm: The Authorised History of MI5*, the differences were only settled after the failure of further high-level discussions held in London and the Far East, when the Colonial Office gave its approval to Sillitoe's proposals.[8] This could only lead inexorably to the winding up of the MSS and the re-establishment of separate Singapore and Kuala Lumpur Special Branches, which would be part of their respective police forces, as had been the case pre-war.

The "Centre" Meets the "Periphery"

As far as it is known, Dalley only met Sillitoe once, and that was when Sillitoe was staying with the Singapore Governor Sir Franklin Gimson on his way through to Australia where he was to advise the Australian Prime Minister on the establishment of the Australian Security Intelligence Service. According to the Governor's Secretary, Christopher Blake, Dalley was "irritated" at the way he thought he had been "sent for to meet Sillitoe to provide him with a briefing on what the MSS had been doing", and he referred to Sillitoe as a "Glasgow corner boy", or a good-for-nothing loafer or idler, or words to that effect. When this remark somehow reached the ears of Sillitoe, he was incensed by what Dalley was reported to have said, especially as he was rather sensitive about his social background as he had not come from the usual privileged Oxford or Cambridge circles of most MI5 officers at the time, had little previous intelligence experience, and had worked his way up through the police ranks as a trooper in the South African police before returning to the UK.[9]

Before the meeting started, which was attended by Sir Franklin Gimson the Singapore Governor and his Secretary Blake, Sillitoe "confronted a startled Dalley with his alleged remarks" and refused to start the meeting until Dalley had tendered an apology. Blake wrote that he had "seldom witnessed so tense a scene", and it was obvious that the head of Britain's MI5 and Dalley, the head of MSS in Singapore, had not got off to a good start, which did very little to mend the strains in relation that had already begun to develop between the two men and their intelligence organizations.[10]

Notes

1. Secret, FCO 141/14360, Colonial Office, Malaya, no. 40, 2 September

1946, telegram to Governor-General, the Honorable Malcolm MacDonald, copied to the Governor, Singapore, and the Governor Malayan Union.
2. Ibid.
3. At the end of his term as Head/SIFE, John Percival (Jack) Morton, CMG, OBE, Indian Police Medal for Gallantry, was offered the appointment of Director of Intelligence, Malaya, by General Templer, then High Commissioner and Director of Operations, Malaya (1952–54), and on his acceptance arrangements were made for him to be temporarily seconded from MI5 to take up the appointment.
4. See A.N. Shaw, "MI5 and the Cold War in South-East Asia: Examining the Performance of Security Intelligence Far East (SIFE), 1946–1963", *Intelligence and National Security*, 2017, "Table 1. Heads of SIFE, 1946–1963", pp. 797–816.
5. Sir Ralph Hone was Secretary General to the Governor General of Malaya (Malcolm MacDonald) 1946–48, Deputy Commissioner-General for Southeast Asia 1948–49, and Governor of British North Borneo 1948–52. Dalley's correspondence with Hone is contained in the *J.D. Dalley Papers*, Rhodes House Library, Top Secret, MSS Ind. Ocn. S.254 (2), "Dalley to Sir Ralph Hone, KBE, MC, TD, Ed, Governor General's Office, Singapore".
6. See *Annual Report of the Singapore Police Force 1946*.
7. Leon Comber, *Singapore Chronicles: Japanese Occupation* (Singapore: Institute of Policy Studies, National University of Singapore/Straits Times Press, 2017) pp. 38–39.
8. Christopher Andrew, *The Defence of the Realm: The Authorised History of MI5* (London: Penguin Books, 2010), p. 448.
9. Sir Percy Sillitoe (22 May 1888 – 1962) came from a police background. He was Director of MI5 from May 1946 to 1953. He had served as a trooper in the South African Mounted Police (circa 1911), Political Officer in Tanganyika (1916–22), and eventually returned to the UK to become Chief Constable Glasgow (1943) and then Sheffield. He was appointed Chief Constable Kent, before becoming Director MI5 in 1946. In 1965 he became the first former Director MI5 to publish

an autobiography, *Cloak without Dagger*. Following his retirement from MI5 he became the head of the International Diamond Security Organisation.
10. Christopher Blake, *A View from Within: The Last Years of British Rule in South-East Asia* (Somerset: Mendip, 1990), p. 89.

Chapter 4

Dalley's Return to Singapore

Lieutenant Colonel Dalley returned to Singapore after the war on 5 February 1947 by the *Empress of Australia* from England. He was met at the wharf by some former members of Dalforce who had served under him in the battle for Singapore. Dalley asked them to gather around him and he told them:

> This is the moment for which I have waited for many years — when I can see and talk to you again. The enemy we fought against has now been defeated but in the world, there are still many unseen forces that are causing unrest.
>
> We must continue, each and every one of us, to maintain peace and security in this country, and I am sure that as in the past, so in the future, you will do your best to attain this end.[1]

Many observers believed he was referring to the beginning of the Cold War (1945–90) and the rise of Communism after WWII as a result of the fundamentally different ideologies and interests between the Soviet Union and the West, which eventually spread to every part of the world. Thus, "Cold War", as opposed to an "atomic hot war", became a term used to indicate the struggle for the hearts and minds of the people between the competing political systems of Communism and Democracy. Essentially, in the Malayan archipelago and Indonesia in particular, this was emphasized to some extent by the power vacuum left by the sudden surrender of the Japanese at the end of WWII after the dropping of the two atomic bombs, but whether this is what Dalley had in mind when he spoke is unclear.

The long *PIJ Supplements* that Dalley wrote after his return to Malaya on "Malay and Indonesian Communists" and the "Indonesian Situation and Malaya" attached to the MSS *Political Intelligence Journals* nos. 5 and 10, which will be referred to later in this study, nevertheless confirm Dalley's growing awareness of the problems which MSS would have to face in dealing with the post-war security situation, including the long-standing threat posed to Malaya's security by Indonesian left-wing parties stirring up trouble with Malay left-wing parties to rise up against British colonialism in Malaya as the Indonesians had done against the Dutch in Indonesia.

It is probably not generally realized that, outside the Soviet Union and China, the Indonesian Communist Party, Partai Komunis Indonesia (PKI), was in terms of numbers one of the largest communist parties in the world. It had a firm base in various Indonesian mass organizations, such as the "All Indonesian Central Labour Organisation", "People's Youth", the "Indonesian Women's Movement", and so on. At its peak it was reliably estimated to have a membership of around 72 million supporters, which represented about one fifth of the total Indonesian population at the time, and it seemed to be able to mix politics with religion.[2]

Indonesian immigration and influence in Malaya had, in fact, been a feature of the demographic structure of several Malay States for centuries. Indonesian immigrants managed to play an important role in Johor at one time and played a notable part, too, in the development of Selangor. Malaya is so close to Indonesia that it was difficult to prevent the migration of Indonesians there.[3] The two countries are separated only by the narrow Straits of Melaka, Indonesians and Malays look alike, most Indonesians were fellow Muslims, the Indonesian language Bahasa Indonesia is little different to Bahasa Melayu (although it is claimed to be more developed and refined), and Indonesians can easily merge with the Malay population. As Colin Abraham points out, there were large influxes of Indonesians into Malaya during the colonial period. In some Malay States they established themselves as rubber smallholders in the supply chain developed by foreign enterprises, but, as many of these links were disrupted during the Japanese Occupation, they moved into towns to find a living, and many of them then took an active part in the new Malay political movements which came into existence known as the "Malay Left".[4]

While Dalley was a "Malay Specialist" and not a "Chinese specialist", and was indeed often criticized for not forewarning the British colonial authorities of the outbreak of the First Malayan Emergency (1948–60) when the Malayan Communist Party (MCP), a Malayan-Chinese party, took up arms to overthrow the British colonial government, the records nevertheless show he was in fact aware of the threat posed by Communism in Malaya, and he spoke openly against it at a special conference convened by Malcolm MacDonald at his headquarters at Phoenix Park, Singapore,[5] on 26 June 1947, a year before the Communist uprising started.

The conference was attended by Sir Edward Gent, Governor, Malayan Union; the Officer Administering the Singapore Government; the Commander-in-Chief, British Southeast Asia Land Forces; the Naval Commander-in-Chief; Major P.H. Winterborn, the acting Director of SIFE; and other senior government officials.

It was opened by Malcolm MacDonald, Britain's seniormost representative in Southeast Asia, with the arresting phrase: "Communism is Enemy Number One in these territories and Southeast Asia." He expounded on the rise of Communism in post-war Malaya and Southeast Asia based on his own observations during his stay in Southeast Asia, and stressed the necessity for counter-intelligence measures to be taken against the MCP before it was too late. Dalley supported MacDonald's speech and spoke at some length on the threat posed by Communism in Malaya and Singapore.[6]

Dalley, who was one of the keynote speakers at the conference, strongly reinforced MacDonald's comments and traced in detail the MCP's efforts in Singapore/Malaya to penetrate trade unions and Malayan political organizations such as the Malay Nationalist Party (MNP), the Malayan Democratic Union (MDU), and other left-wing political bodies.

In fact, in the three years after the end of the war, leading up to the MCP uprising in June 1948, there were several left-wing political parties that were of interest to the MSS, including the MNP, the MDU and the Malayan Indian Congress (MIC), and in his talk Dalley revealed that the MCP had seeded the MNP with a large donation of funds at the end of WWII.[7]

MacDonald suggested that the Kuomintang — then engaged in an internecine struggle with the Chinese Communist Party (CCP) for the control of China, which was only settled in the CCP's favour in 1949 — could perhaps be made more use of to fight the MCP's uprising in Malaya. But Gent, the Malayan Governor, supported by the Secretary of Chinese Affairs, Malaya, did not favour this suggestion, and took the view that the government should not be seen to support any political party.

By the end of 1948, the first year of the Malayan Emergency, as a result of security measures taken by the government, only the

United Malays National Organisation (UMNO) and the MIC of the existing Malayan political parties survived. The MCP itself was proscribed on 23 July 1948, and four other political parties with Communist connections were simultaneously banned, viz., MPAJA Ex-Servicemen's Association, New Democratic Youth League, Ikatan Pemudah Tanah Ayer (PETA; a Malay youth movement), and the Indian New Democratic Youth League.

At the conference, Dalley referred to the MCP's overseas' links, particularly with China and Russia, and reported that three MCP representatives had been sent to attend the recent British Conference of British Empire Communist Parties in London, the Second Empire Conference of Communists and Workers Parties convened by the British Communist Party, which was not a proscribed party in the UK. They were Wu Tien Wang; the Malay Abdul Rashid bin Maidin (also known as Rashid Mydin); and the Indian R.G. Balan. On his return to Malaya the following year (1948), Balan was arrested by the Malayan Special Branch for instigating labour unrest on rubber estates in Perak, and eventually detained for ten years under the newly promulgated Emergency Regulations. Wu Tien Wang, who was undoubtedly a dedicated Communist (although prepared to criticize what he perceived to be MCP shortcomings), survived the Malayan Emergency only to be executed in an "internal purge" by the MCP's North Malayan Bureau in south Thailand in early 1969.[8]

In September 1947, after the conference, Dalley wrote to Gent to urge him to take "action against armed Communists training and encamping in the jungle", and he provided in support of his report the locations of several of the communist camps. He estimated there were 5,000 "activists", by which he meant armed members of the MCP who had gone underground and taken to the jungle, and 250,000 supporters (known in Chinese as *Min*

Yuen or "People's Movement"), and other Communist supporters among the Chinese population in towns and villages throughout the country. The figure of "activists", he said, was based on reliable information obtained by the MSS, while the estimate of 250,000 that he provided was an estimate of Communist supporters on the jungle fringes whose members went about their normal livelihoods as farmers, rubber tappers, tin miners and so on by day but were available to provide support to the MCP when required at other times. As it turned out, Dalley's figures were uncannily close to the government's own estimates of the MCP's strength that were published a year or so later.

While Dalley had always considered that the MCP was one of the main targets of the MSS, he must nevertheless have been handicapped to some extent, as the only European officer in the MSS who could speak Chinese, that is, the Cantonese dialect, was Ian S. Wylie. However, he could probably obtain information about the MCP from Lai Teck, the Secretary General of the MCP, who since pre-war had been a secret agent of the Singapore SB, as well as Khaw Kai Boh, an officer then in the Singapore SB who was extremely well-informed of both Kuomintang and MCP activities.

In fact it was rumoured that when Lai Teck, who in his time had worked as an agent for French intelligence in French Indo-China, the Singapore Special Branch, and the Japanese Kempeitai — on the verge in 1947 of being accused of being a traitor and brought to justice by the MCP Central Committee — decided to decamp with most of the MCP's funds, he was given refuge in an MSS/SB safe house in Singapore before leaving for Hong Kong under one of his many assumed names, although this rumour has not so far been substantiated.

Eventually, Lai Teck was tracked down in Thailand by Chin Peng, who had taken over the leadership of the MCP, and strangled to death when he put up resistance to being detained by a party of Thai and Vietnamese Communists who had been sent to arrest him and bring him back to Malaya to face his accusers in the MCP. There is no record, however, of what happened to the MCP's funds (currency and jewellery) which he is alleged to have taken with him.[9]

While Gent was reluctant to take action on Dalley's report on the MCP, he referred the matter to the Malayan Commissioner of Police, H.B. Langworthy, who was on the verge of retiring on medical grounds, and the British Residents of Johor and Perak. The Malayan Chief Secretary replied on behalf of the Governor to Dalley's report and said the matter had been investigated and no unusual activities had been found to support his report.

According to Dalley, he continued to advocate the co-ordination of action by the security forces against the MCP throughout Malaya and Singapore, and recommended that known "open" and "secret" Communist offices throughout the country should be raided by the police, and the police and military should attack Communist camps located in the jungle. Dalley maintained that although the Singapore Government was willing to take action on his reports, and the Governor General, Malcolm MacDonald, supported him, Gent refused to accept the veracity of his reports.[10]

In December 1947, Dalley wrote that he was desperate that no action was being taken by Gent on his reports, and he wrote "three pages of Gent's omissions and commissions" and sent them to Gent, with a copy to MacDonald. In April 1948, he continued, "a number of [Communist] conferences were held when it was obvious to everybody that an uprising was about to take place. However, Singapore took independent action on April 14th but the Malayan Union still refused to cooperate or coordinate."

However, Dalley wrote that when he subsequently visited the British Resident in Ipoh, Perak, during the first part of 1948, the latter then admitted that the information Dalley had provided was correct.

To conclude, at midnight on 20 June 1948, the British colonial government declared war on the MCP's uprising, which became known as the First Malayan Emergency, and a series of Emergency Regulations were promulgated that provided the government with extraordinary powers to combat the armed uprising, including the death penalty for the unlawful possession of firearms, ammunition, or explosives. The writ of habeas corpus was suspended and authorized police officers were conferred with wide powers of arrest and detention. Later in the Emergency, the restrictions were intensified and the movement of foodstuffs and other essential supplies were controlled and the population was issued with identity cards.

On 26 June 1948, the Secretary of State for the Colonies recalled Gent to London for what were described diplomatically as "consultations". But MacDonald had, in fact, earlier reported adversely on him to the Secretary of State, and his report had been supported by the British Army's Commander-in-Chief for the Far East and the Air Officer Commanding Malaya. MacDonald's main complaint was that Gent had failed to estimate the seriousness of the situation and appreciate the challenge to law and order posed by the MCP or to deal with complaints about the incompetence of the Malayan Police higher command, and had ignored warnings he had been given by Dalley about the impending Communist uprising, which posed a serious threat to British colonial rule.

The last conference Gent attended before he departed for London was held at MacDonald's residence at Bukit Serene in Johor Baru in early June 1948. According to Dalley, Gent was "very subdued" on this occasion. He asked to see Dalley privately, and then, according to Dalley, "he produced from his attaché case the memorandum I had written on his omissions and commissions and went through it paragraph by paragraph, admitted to it all, and asked me if we could continue to be friends. As we shook hands on it, I felt quite emotional but my main feeling was one of relief that when he reached London he would give full support to all-out action. It was sad that he did not reach London."[11]

It was understood that Gent would resign on arrival at London, but tragically the RAF York transport aircraft on which he was travelling collided with a Scandinavian Airlines Skymaster airliner on its approach to London airport and crashed. All on board the two aircraft were killed.

Notes

1. *Straits Times*, 6 February 1947.
2. See "Communist Party of Indonesia", Wikipedia (accessed 20 October 2017).
3. Colin Abraham, *"The Finest Hour": The Malaysian-MCP Peace Accord in Perspective* (Petaling Jaya: SIRD, 2006), pp. 12–13.
4. Ibid.
5. Phoenix Park still exists as a place name on Tanglin Road, Singapore, for the area built on a slight hillside which was the headquarters of Malcolm MacDonald when he was British Governor General (later Commissioner-General) for Southeast Asia. However, there is no trace of its former importance and some of its old buildings are now occupied by a few scattered British trading companies and pre-schools. It is unlikely that many people realize nowadays that when it was established after the Japanese surrender in August 1945, its name was taken from the phoenix shoulder flash worn by units of the British Southeast Asia Command in WWII. Admiral Lord Louis Mountbatten, the Commander-in-Chief of the British Southeast Asia Command in WWII, however, established his own headquarters in

the Cathay Building, Singapore, after the Japanese surrender, as did MacDonald before moving his headquarters to Phoenix Park.
6. Top Secret, *J.D. Dalley Papers*, Rhodes House Library, Oxford, MSS. Ind. Ocn. S. 254, "Special Conference held under the Chairmanship of H.E. the Governor-General in South East Asia, on 26 June 1947", contained in J.D. Dalley, "Threat of Communism in Malaya and Singapore 1947".
7. Ibid. This report does not appear to have been referred to by Anthony Short. See CAB 128/13, CM 52 (48) 5, "Proscription of the Malayan Communist Party"; and Cheah Boon Kheng, "Some Aspects of the Malayan Emergency: 1948–1960", in *The History of South-East, South and East Asia: Essays and Documents*, edited by Khoo Kay Kim (Kuala Lumpur: Oxford University Press, 1977), pp. 111–23.

It is not generally known that the MSS maintained files, too, on non-Communist political parties of "security interest", such as the Kuomintang and even UMNO, the leading Malay political party that had been formed by Dato Onn bin Ja'afar.
8. Dato Sri C.C. Too's Papers SP127/A/3, "Notes on the History of the Malayan Communist Party", University of Malaya Library, p. 120. See also John Josiah Coe, *Beautiful Flowers and Poisonous Weeds, Problems of Historicism, Ethics and Internal Antagonism, the Case of the MCP* (PhD Dissertation [restricted], University of Queensland, 1993), pp. 174–75.
9. For information about Lai Teck, see Yoji Akashi, "Lai Teck, Secretary General of the Malayan Communist Party, 1939–1947", *Journal of the South Seas Society* 49, pt. 1 (June 1996): 1–20; and Leon Comber, "Traitor of all Traitors — Secret Agent *Extraordinaire*: Lai Teck, Secretary-General; Malayan Communist Party (1939–1947)", *Journal of the Malayan Branch Royal Asiatic Society* 83, pt. 2, no. 299 (December 2010): 1–29. See also C.F. Yong, *The Origins of Malayan Communism* (Singapore: South Seas Society, 1997), p. 193.

Lai Teck was accused by the MCP of embezzling the following party funds: $290,000 in Japanese currency notes issued during the Occupation of Malaya, 170 gold coins, and 23 taels of gold. Further, in the post-war years he was alleged to have misappropriated Party funds amounting to $130,000 (Straits dollars).

Khaw Kai Boh (b. 1918), an interesting character in his own right, served first as an MSS Inspector and then as an Assistant Superintendent of Police in the Malayan Special Branch before resigning from the police to study law in London. When he was in Kuala Lumpur, he shared an office with the author at Special Branch federal headquarters. Before WWII he had been an Assistant Boarding Officer, Chinese Protectorate, Singapore (1939), and immediately after the Japanese surrender in August 1945 he was seconded to a British army field security unit at SEAC HQ (1945–46), before joining the MSS. When the People's Action Party (PAP) came to power in Singapore, he was in the Singapore SB, and after being warned that he was *persona non grata* by the PAP, probably due to his dabbling in local politics and allegedly being involved in business activities, he resigned and left Singapore for Malaya. He joined the Malayan Chinese Association (MCA) and became a junior minister in Prime Minister Tunku Abdul Rahman's government. He died not long afterwards.

10. Gent was not alone in ignoring the warnings he had been given by Dalley. J.B. Williams, Assistant Under-Secretary of State, Colonial Office, minuted on 24 May 1948 that he did not think that any information had reached the CO's Eastern Department "that would lead us to suppose that any serious trouble is brewing in Malaya": CO 537/4733, minuted by J.B. Williams and G.F. Seel, 28–31 May 1948.

11. Top Secret, *J.D. Dalley Papers*, Rhodes House Library, Oxford, MSS. Ind. Ocn. S 234.

Chapter 5

The Indonesian Situation and Malaya[1]

When Dalley was confident that the serious threat posed by the MCP to overthrow British rule in Malaya, which he had long persisted in reporting, had at last been officially recognized and was being dealt with by the government, he turned his attention to another security problem that was beginning to emerge in the Malayan Peninsula. Indonesian left-wing elements were making determined efforts to induce Malay nationalist and left-wing political parties — many of them having maintained contact over time either directly or through the considerable number of Indonesians who had settled in Malaya — to rise up against British rule and resist the return of the British to Malaya, as the Indonesians had done to the Dutch in Indonesia.

In fact, as Dalley well appreciated, if they had succeeded, it was quite possible the Malay nationalist and left-wing parties would join forces with the MCP to present a united Malay-Chinese front to fight against British colonial rule in Malaya, which would have placed the British in a much more difficult situation than they faced in fighting the MCP alone when the Malayan Emergency was declared in June 1948.

The Japanese had virtually "given" independence to Indonesia in the confused period shortly before they surrendered, when Sukarno and Hatta declared independence on 17 August 1945, leading to the establishment of the Indonesian Republic under Sukarno as President. As rumours of the Japanese surrender filtered through to the people of Singapore/Malaya, Malay nationalists also intended to declare independence at the same time, and it is said that the Malay nationalist leader Mustapha Hussain wept bitterly as the Japanese surrender forestalled the declaration of independence for Malaya by just forty-eight hours, thus destroying the dream of a greater Malay nation.[2]

However, in Indonesia the political situation was soon overshadowed by the fighting that took place between the Indonesian Republican forces, who were impatient and determined to wrest independence for Indonesia from the returning Dutch colonial power by force rather than negotiation. Matters were further complicated by the arrival of a brigade of the 23rd British Indian Infantry Division, sent by the British from Singapore to assist in the evacuation of Dutch civilians who had been interned by the Japanese during the war. It was intended that the brigade should remain neutral and not become involved in the conflict. However, the brigade soon became caught up in the uprising when its commander was killed in a confrontation with the Indonesian Republican forces.[3]

The brunt of the fighting on the Indonesian side was borne by the Indonesian Youth Corps, the Pemoeda Rahasia Indonesia, rather than the more disciplined Indonesian Tentera Keslamat Rakjat (Peace Preservation Army), which favoured obtaining independence from Dutch colonial rule by a diplomatic approach rather than military means.[4]

An agreement of sorts was reached between the Dutch and the Republican forces, known as the Linggadjati Agreement, by which the Dutch recognized the Indonesian Republic as the de facto authority in Java, Madura and Sumatra. But without going into the most involved situation which developed when the Dutch started what they referred to as "police actions" against the Republican forces and the UN Security Council established a Committee of Good Offices which led to the signing of another agreement in January 1948, the Renville Agreement, on board the USS *Renville* anchored off Jakarta, which would take us far from the subject of this book, sharp military clashes continued between the Dutch and Indonesian Republican forces until well into 1948 and 1949. As Yong Mun Cheong states in his study *The Indonesian Revolution and the Singapore Connection 1945–1949*, "The negotiations which ensued from the 1948 military actions were collectively called the Round Table Conference and began on 23 August 1949 in The Hague. Sovereignty was finally transferred to Indonesia on 27 December 1949, though not in the form that the Republic wanted. Instead of a unitary state under the Republic of Indonesia, a federal state (the United States of Indonesia) was constructed."[5]

Even so, the international situation remained unclear. The UK objected to the decision to admit an Indonesian representative to the United Nations on the grounds that the Republic of Indonesia was not recognized as an independent state. The US offers of mediation were rejected by the Republicans but accepted by the Dutch, who maintained that the matter was outside the jurisdiction of the United Nations. The Russian delegate accused the UK and the United States of complicity with the Dutch and alleged that as colonial powers they were both primarily concerned with their own business interests in Indonesia. Dr Van Mook pressed his Cabinet,[6] which itself was divided on the issue, for permission to continue with what he termed "police action" in Indonesia, and both sides of the fighting in

Indonesia, the Republicans and the Dutch, were allegedly accused of contravening the "cease-fire" orders.[7]

Meanwhile, as Dalley observed, the situation in Malaya from 1945 to 1947 had already become complicated by the profusion of secret Indonesian agents who seemed to have no problem in entering Malaya/Singapore from Indonesia. To make matters worse, many of the senior British immigration officers had been killed during the war or had been medically boarded out and their places taken by less experienced Malay officers who did not see the importance of preventing Indonesians — who followed the same religion, spoke more or less the same language, and looked the same as them — entering Malaya.

From this point of view, many of Dalley's reports in the *Political Intelligence Journal* of the MSS from early 1946 to mid-1948 of the activities of political Indonesian influences in Malaya are often insightful, especially as the situation was to become a matter of serious security concern to the British colonial authorities, and no longer, as described by some of his critics, Dalley's "obsession".

In 1947, Dalley had prepared a chart with a key to Communist and left-wing Indonesian and Malayan political movements (see appendix 1), which he had originally prepared for the talk he gave at a conference on "Communism in Malaya" organized by Malcolm MacDonald, the British Commissioner-General for Southeast Asia, at the Commissioner-General's offices at Phoenix Park on 26 June 1947.

As Dalley opined in his presentation, "It is a popular belief that there was no political consciousness among Malays prior to the Japanese war", but, as he correctly pointed out, "the seeds were sown which were now bearing fruit in the situation which now confronted the MSS in the Malayan peninsula." While Dalley did not claim to present a complete historical picture of the connection between Indonesian and Malay left-wing parties, it is nevertheless a valuable record of the problem which he felt the MSS then faced.

Dalley's presentation is useful as it provides a historical sweep of Indonesian and Malay left-wing parties from early times to 1948. Whilst he did not claim it was complete, it does at least provide a general idea of the close contacts between Indonesian and Malayan left-wing parties, which is not easily available elsewhere. Accordingly, an attempt has been made, too, in this chapter to provide some idea of the information he provided in the two supplements he prepared, viz., Supplement to *PIJ* no. 10/47 (BAM 11/8), "Indonesian Situation and Malaya", dated 30 June 1947, and Supplement no. 5 to *PIJ* no. 11/48 (BAM 11/8), "Malay and Indonesian Communists", dated 15 June 1948, even going back a little into the past to do so.[8]

Kesatuan Melayu Muda (KMM) and the Origins of the MNP

The Kesatuan Melayu Muda (KMM) was first registered as an association in 1938. Its President was Ibrahim bin Haji Ya'acob. It is opportune to mention it briefly here for the purpose of this narrative to establish how the important Malay Nationalist Party (MNP), which was to figure often and prominently in Malay politics later, developed from the KMM. The KMM did not qualify for mention as a Communist organization and, in fact, its activities in 1941 seemed to indicate it was on the opposite side. However, it did participate in Japanese fifth column work — and its leader became a self-admitted agent of the Kempeitai — during the Japanese Occupation until it was later suppressed by the Japanese (see below).

As Ishak bin Haji Mohamed, who later became President of the MNP, said in a speech he gave in Johor on 29 April 1946 referring to the origins of the MNP:

The MNP is not a new Party. Its seeds were planted long before the war came to Malaya. It was then known as the KMM Malaya, which was established in 1938. At that time, I was working for the newspaper *Warta Malaya* through which the objects of the KMM was transmitted to the *rayat* (people).

When the Japanese invaded Malaya, the KMM realized that to save the Malays from being treated like the Chinese, its best strategy would be to pretend to cooperate, and its leaders quickly gained the confidence of the Japanese. However, when the Japanese started to ill-treat the Malays, the KMM resisted, and it was disbanded by the Japanese. Many of the KMM members then joined Wataniah, a Malay underground resistance movement in Perak and Pahang, and operated with the MCP's underground army, the "Malayan People's Anti-Japanese Army" (MPAJA).

Union of Indonesian Seamen

Little has actually been written about the subject of Malay and Indonesian "Communists" during 1946, but names that are now fairly well-known to Indonesian scholars do appear from time to time in Dalley's account, such as Mas Alimin, Tan Malaka, Sutan Jenain, Jamaluddin Tamin bin Maiden, and Abdul Rashid bin Maiden. The last-named, in fact, is the "first Malay communist" who is openly associated with the MPAJA, and was one of three delegates, with a Chinese and an Indian, who were sent to represent the MCP at the conference of Empire Communist Parties in London in February 1947.

During his stay in Singapore, according to Dalley, Mas Alimin contacted many prominent Indonesians and on his return to Java claimed to have been successful in establishing "Communist agents" there, although he did not identify who they were. However, he did refer to the Sharikat Pegawai Laot

Indonesia (Union of Indonesian Seamen), which, as early as 1914, claimed to have a membership of twelve thousand seamen working on ships of the Rotterdam Lloyd Co. and the Netherlands Steamship Co., the two leading Dutch steamship companies, which regularly visited Singapore. The head and President of the Central Committee of the Union of Indonesian Seamen in Amsterdam was the well-known Indonesian Communist Semaoen.

In February 1925, according to Dalley's account, the Union of Indonesian Seamen and the People's Partnership had established close connections with each other, and the latter had meanwhile expanded its activities in Malaya by establishing schools and spreading Communist propaganda by informal meetings in Malayan kampongs and towns. The Union had ambitious plans, too, to create a Federation of Indonesian Trade Unions in Indonesia, for which it was reliably reported to have received funding from the Soviet authorities in Moscow and Canton through Tan Malaka, the well-known Indonesian Comintern agent. As Dalley commented, this state of affairs in a country like Indonesia, adjacent to Malaya, with a daily flow of travellers between the two countries, made it almost impossible for Malays to avoid the propaganda that was being put out by Indonesian Communist and left-wing elements.[9]

Central Committee of the Chinese, Japanese, Australian, Indo-Chinese and Javanese Communist Parties

According to Dalley's report, based on an A1 source, the highest intelligence grading, instructions had been received from Moscow in 1925 calling for an increase in Communist propaganda in Southeast Asia.

Izvestia, the leading official Soviet newspaper commented at the time that it would "awaken a race [referring to Malays] which has hitherto slept a sound sleep while playing a significant part in the world's economy...."

The "instructions" probably referred to an ambitious proposal by the Third International to form a Central Committee of the Chinese, Japanese, Australian, Indo-Chinese and Javanese Communist Parties. Meanwhile, the Malayan Special Branch was successful in obtaining a copy of the report which was prepared in 1925 by Tan Malaka urging the establishment of an appropriate organization for communication with the Comintern; the despatch of "comrades" conversant with local Chinese dialects in Southeast Asia; and the creation of a "special school for the Malayan population". This would certainly seem to be a very ambitious proposal, but it does not appear that anything came of it.

Tan Malaka's Report on Malaya

Tan Malaka visited Singapore in early November 1925 and the following extract from a letter he wrote which was intercepted by the Singapore Special Branch postal unit about his stay is worth noting, as it revealed that not very much progress had been made in propagating Communism among the Malay community:

> So far not the slightest advantage is to be seen from the work of our "dealers" [contacts?] in [Singapore?] or [Penang?]. You may say they are quite incapable, but in criticising them it must not be forgotten that proper inhabitants there, who form only a minority, are all conservative in their manner of living and thinking and are petty bourgeois. On the departure of Hadji Moek from [Singapore?] his kindness was invoked to make a visit to the F.M.S. The impressions which he obtained everywhere did not differ from those gained from [Singapore?] and [Penang?]. The section of the population which understands [economy?] and [politics?] are the [Chinese?]. In the harbours, in buildings,

in the trains, and above all in commerce, the Chinese are the most prominent. None-the-less their federation is very weak.

You will understand that in these circumstances it is impossible to effect a union. The railway personnel and those in establishments connected with the railway are all *Klings*.[10] In these circles no beginning has been made to set up any association. There is not a single daily paper in the Straits or F.M.S. that is read by Malays. In brief, if one looks for a movement in the F.M.S., it is not to be sought from the side of the Malays. It will certainly come from the Chinese and *Klings*, whatever sort of movement it may be.

Dalley, again quoting an A1 source, confirmed that Tan Malaka after stopping over in Penang had visited 84 Onan Road, Singapore, occupied by a certain Abdul Ghaffar bin Abdul Rahman, a Javanese pilgrim broker, which was used as a secret underground Communist-front correspondence address, and by March 1926 the Singapore Special Branch became aware that four well-known Javanese Communists — Moeso, Winanta, Boedisoejitro, and Soebakat — were living in Singapore. By that time, Tan Malaka had moved to Chiengmai from Penang and the 84 Onan Road Communist correspondence address referred to above had been replaced by 709 North Bridge Road, Singapore, where letters were addressed to a non-existent "Tuan Moechtar".

1926 Revolution in Java

On 12 November 1926, a significant Communist uprising occurred in West Java, which became known as the 1926 Revolution, and Dalley provided the following brief account of the uprising and its developments, which he felt, as he said, would be of interest if a similar situation were ever to arise in Malaya.[11]

On the night of 12 November, a Communist uprising occurred in West Java, simultaneous disturbances took place in Batavia, in several villages in the Preanger and many districts of Bantam. In Batavia itself small bodies of armed natives attacked two of the gaols with the object of liberating the prisoners but they were easily driven off.

A party of Communists also seized the telephone exchange in Lower Batavia, but were dispersed the following morning before any real damage had been done to the installation. In Batavia itself the situation by Saturday morning was completely in hand.

The main disturbances occurred in the various small towns in Bantam where the native population turned out in large numbers, attacked police stations and destroyed telegraph wires and bridges. In this district three or four officials were killed and a Dutch Eurasian railway employee murdered, whilst an appeal had evidently been made to the religious feelings of the mob, as in some cases gangs were dressed in white, symbolic of preparedness for martyrdom. Owing to the more general nature of the rising in Bantam, troops had to be employed for the suppression of the movement, and it is reported that some 300 rebels were killed during the course of operations.

Elsewhere occasional attacks were made on police patrols, as a result of which several policemen were killed, telephone and telegraph wires were cut, and cases of incendiarism occurred.

These disorders, as well as the more minor ones which took place in Mid and East Java were, however, easily suppressed.

The rebels, for the most part, were armed with *parangs*, cutting knives, whilst many of the leaders carried firearms, especially automatics of a variety that can be purchased easily at any seaport in the East from the crews of steamers trading to Europe.

Except in Bantam, where the rising was of a more popular character, the small gangs of Communists appeared to be completely in the hands of their local leaders, and came out mainly because they were ordered to do so, whilst as often as not they had laid down their arms with alacrity at the command of numerically insignificant bodies of government officials or police.

It would appear that as if the majority of the thinking coolies, miscalled Communists, who took part in the rising, had been hypnotised in the belief that they merely had to come out in open resistance to the government to succeed in overthrowing it and no further action would be necessary except to enjoy the fruits of their daring.

As soon as the authorities realised the seriousness of the outbreak and the cause of it, they immediately took steps to arrest every known leader of the Communist Party [PKI] in the whole country, whether concerned with the outbreak or not, a proceeding which had a most salutary effect. Owing to the well-known wish of the [Dutch] Governor-General, little harshness was employed in making arrests, and in fact, even in the suppression of rebels in arms, [the Dutch] claimed that firing was only resorted to in the last extremity when capture by any other method was out of the question.

The total number of Communists arrested by the end of November had reached several hundreds who were to be dealt with by special tribunals, and if guilty, banished to a new Penal Settlement in New Guinea. Those who had taken part in the actual rising, however, were to be punished in the first instance by the local Courts before banishment took place.

There can be no doubt that the P.K.I. [in Java] was behind the outbreak as evidenced by the organised fashion of the uprising, the secrecy with which the plans were laid out, and the choice of the birthday of Sun Yat Sen as the day on which the rising was to occur.... Although the outbreak has been completely quelled and the Communist Party has received a severe setback, unless something is done to remove the underlying causes of the revolt it can only be a question of time before a new and stronger National Party arises, wise in the knowledge of past defeats and conscious of the immense power which can be exerted by an organised proletariat even if it does not resort to arms for victory.[12]

However, from an examination of the correspondence of Communist leaders in 1925, it is apparent that Tan Malaka, an Indonesian and by far the shrewdest of them, was actually opposed to the revolt in 1926 on the grounds that he felt it was premature. Dalley commented, and probably correctly, "It must be realised that from the outset that although great stress was laid by the Dutch authorities on the Communist nature of the revolt, the real force behind it was the Nationalist movement and a dislike for European domination. With the exception of a mere handful of native leaders who had been in contact with European and Russian Communists and may be supposed to have assimilated some of the doctrines, the ordinary member of the P.K.I. is entirely ignorant of the articles of the Communist faith."

The Adat Perpateh

As many districts in Negri Sembilan and Malacca are heavily populated by Minangkabau Malays, the following notes made by Dalley on the situation in Indonesia will be of interest as they refer to the "Adat Perpateh" of the Minangkabau Malays:

> Even after the putting down of the actual disturbances there have been repeated rumours of fresh plots against the administration, although in no instance have any of these reports materialised. It is becoming clear that Communist agitation, though it was certainly the immediate, was not the only, or the ultimate cause of the rising in this district, where antagonism towards the Government has always been latent. This antagonism arises

in large measure out of the opposition, dating back many years past, of the more progressive section of the local population [the Minangkabau Malays] to the curious system of matriarchal succession and of the common possession of family property which still continues to be observed in their midst. Years ago, the Dutch Government, in order to strengthen its hold upon the country, chose to take the side of the holders of tradition in this matter. The result has been that in a sense, the administration has become involved in the fierce disputes around the question at issue, and that it has incurred the hostility of these (including orthodox Moslem supporters of the Islamic law of succession) who demand the abolition or at least the mitigation, of an archaic survival of tribal rule which is felt to be in accord neither with the social conditions of today, nor with the precepts of the Koran.

Dalley continued, "true to their customary policy, the communists seized upon these elements of discontent and utilised them for the purpose of fomenting an insurrection".

On 18 December 1928, Moeso and Mas Alimin, two of the organizers of the revolt in Java, were arrested in Singapore by the Singapore Special Branch, but a banishment enquiry revealed that though these two men, and through them the revolutionary party in the Netherlands East Indies, were directly connected with Moscow, they themselves had not carried out any subversive activities in Malaya. They were consequently released and left almost immediately for Canton.

World Federation of Trade Unions (WFTU)

Alimin next came to attention representing Java at the Pan Pacific Labour Conference at Hangchow in May 1927, together with other representatives such as Tom Mann, representing Great Britain, Earle Browder, representing the United States, and several

Russians, one of whom, Ismailov, passed a resolution to form the "World Federation of Trade Unions (WFTU)". In February 1928, the peripatetic Alimin was said to be in Shanghai, using his Chinese pseudonym "Ho Ming Lie", and in May 1928 he was reported to be active propagating communism among Malay and Indonesian students at the Al Azhar University in Cairo.

About the middle of 1928, a branch of the "League against Imperialism" was opened in Singapore, and it was reliably reported by the Singapore Special Branch that Alimin and another Javanese, a Malay, an Indian and several Chinese had joined forces with the local Communist Party. Two Malay-language newspapers, *Pilehan Timor* (Choice of the East) and *Seruan Azhar* (Voice of Azhar), published by the students, were distributed in Malaya.

However, as Dalley points out, the desire of communist agitators to foster the growth of their ideology among the Malays and Indonesians in Malaya did not meet with much success, and what little progress had been made up to the end of 1928 to develop communism came from efforts made by the Chinese Hainanese community.[13]

The first Congress of the League against Imperialism held in Brussels in February 1927 was in fact sponsored by the Soviet Union, and one of the resolutions passed was "A general amnesty to be granted for the recent insurrection in the Netherland East Indies".

The Partai Komunis Indonesia, referred to earlier, had meanwhile been suppressed by the Dutch as a political body, and it was reported to have split into small groups, study clubs, and religious parties under different names, which were difficult to detect, and secret plans were made for a second revolution by the PKI to take place on 17 July 1927.[14] The Dutch authorities, however, were forewarned and suppressed the revolt in Batavia. It was suspected that Moscow was behind this latest attempt, and the presence of the elder statesman Mohammad Hatta, who was known to be pro-Russian, was accepted as evidence of Soviet influence and support. Hatta was on the "Executive Council of the League against Imperialism", or, to give it its full title, "The League against Imperialism and Colonisation and for National Liberties", and later became Prime Minister of the Republic of Indonesia.

The South Seas Communist Party

In June 1928 it became apparent that strong Communist influences were active among Malay students at the ancient Al Azhar University in Cairo. The students apparently published two newspapers in Malay, the *Pilehan Timor* and *Seruan Azhar*, referred to previously, which followed an anti-British line. About the middle of 1928 a branch of the "The League against Imperialism and Colonisation and for National Liberties" was formed in Singapore, and there were good reasons to suspect that Alimin and a group of agitators consisting of another Javanese, a Malay, an Indian and several Chinese had joined forces with the local "South Seas Communist Party."[15] The detention by the Singapore Special Branch of a Bugis named "Ali", a sailor on the SS *Van de Parra*, led to the identification of the following members of the Provisional Committee of the South Seas Communist Party:

- Ahmad Baki bin Suib — (see MSS *Political Intelligence Journal* no. 4/48, p. 101)
- Salleh bin Sapi — a Malay from Malacca
- Jamaluddin — a Padang Malay in Singapore
- Emat alias Abdul Hamid — a Javanese in Singapore
- Haji Mahmud bin Hashim — a Padang Malay in Singapore

The members of the Provisional Committee were arrested by the Singapore Special Branch and it was subsequently determined that Ali, Salleh and Haji Mahmud, together with two Chinese Communists, had attended the annual meeting of the Pan-Pacific Trade Union Secretariat in Shanghai in 1929. Haji Mahmud and Ali were identified, too, as revolutionaries prominent in the 1926 revolt in Java.

As Dalley commented, although there were increased reports from October 1930 onwards of Malays being connected with communist activities, it was not nevertheless considered by the authorities that they presented a serious security menace.

Joseph Ducroux alias Serge Le Franc

The most important intelligence development of the time, and undoubtedly an important coup for the Singapore Special Branch as its ramifications were extremely widespread, was the arrest in Singapore on 1 June 1931 by René Onraet, head of the Singapore SB, of the French agent Joseph Ducroux alias Serge le Franc, an agent of the Communist Pan Pacific Trade Union Secretariat in Shanghai.[16] As a result of his arrest the headquarters of the Secretariat were raided by the Shanghai Police Special Branch, which led to the subsequent arrest of Hilaire Noulens, Secretary of the Shanghai Comintern, and the capture of documents of worldwide importance which resulted in the virtual collapse of the Comintern's Far East operations.[17]

Ducroux's interrogation in Singapore provided further intelligence about the names of the entire Comintern network in Southeast Asia and China and led to the arrest in Hong Kong on 10 October 1932, by the Hong Kong Police Special Branch, of Tan Malaka, as well as the arrest in Saigon by the French Sûreté of other Vietnamese Communist leaders.

The above documents revealed a considerable amount of information about Javanese Communists as well as their intended movements throughout Southeast Asia:

- Tan Malaka was to move from Amoy to Rangoon
- Alimin, alias Dirdja, was to follow Tan Malaka
- Moeso was to act as a liaison officer between Tan Malaka and Alimin and the Far Eastern Bureau in Shanghai
- The identity of Bassa, a young, hitherto unknown, Javanese intellectual was revealed. He was a member of the Communist Party who had taken a leading role in the 1926 rebellion in Java, and, after visiting China in 1927, was believed to be in Malaya engaged in the selection and despatch of Malay students to Khabarovsk.

Little is known about the latter activity, its purpose, details of the Malay students involved, or indeed if any were sent at all, and it seems to have escaped the attention of researchers so far. Khabarovsk is a city on the Amur River in the Russian Far East near the Chinese border.

According to Dalley, Tan Malaka said that he was on his way to Burma to meet the leaders of the Partai Republikan Indonesia (PARI) to decide whether the time was ripe for direct action by the PARI, a nationalist body in the Netherlands East Indies with a Javanese and Sumatran following, to rise up against Dutch colonial rule. He denied he was connected with subversive movements directed against the British in Singapore/Malaya. Not surprisingly, he denied, too, the incriminating evidence found in Noulen's papers which seemed to confirm he was in the pay of Moscow.

Dalley commented that Tan Malaka's admission in regard to PARI must be "incomplete" and that it was "impossible" that Tan Malaka's successful launching of the PARI programme would leave Singapore/Malaya, Siam, Indo-China, the Philippines, and possibly Burma, unaffected. The overwhelming history of Tan Malaka's past and present, extending over many years, leaves little doubt that his visit to Burma must have been connected with plans of greater importance than the local aims of PARI, the leaders of which were recruited from the surviving leaders of the old PKI that engineered the 1926 rebellion in Java.

Tan Malaka was banished from Hong Kong, his associate in Hong Kong, Toledo alias Daud, was also banished, and Jamaluddin was banished from Singapore.[18]

Spread of Communism among Malays

In September 1931 there were reported to be five Malays who were members of the Kuala Pilah (Negri Sembilan) Divisional Committee of the Communist Party. The General Labour Union (GLU) claimed an increasing number of Malay "adherents" and announced the publication of a periodical in Malay and Javanese called *Soeara Boeroeh Malaya* (Voice of Malayan Labour). At the same time, a cyclostyled manifesto of the Communist Party in Malay was issued in Terengganu, a predominantly Malay State.

In October 1931, a document entitled "Plan of the Work of the Dutch East Indies Bureau (D.E.I.B)" came into the hands of the Singapore Special Branch. In spite of its impressive title, it was a small organization consisting of three members only: a president, an organizer, and a propagandist. Nevertheless, it had ambitious objects, such "as assisting in all possible ways the work done by the Malayan Communist Party (MCP) in establishing our movement among the Malays"; establishing contact with members of the PKI now underground in Malaya in order to "establish a branch of the P.K.I. in Malaya"; to "send one of our Malay comrades to Indonesia to link up with the P.K.I. there";

to seek connections in Indonesia or "bring together Indonesians living in Malaya to establish either a labour or a peasants union to strengthen our organisation".

The writer of the document was thought to be "Bassa", mentioned earlier, a Hokkien born in Indonesia with the Chinese name Teo Yuen Foo, who passed as a Javanese under the name of Soemito. He was known to use many other aliases, too.

The material for the publication "Voice of Malayan Labour", mentioned earlier, was traced to a document written by Alimin while he was in Shanghai. He, Moeso and Darsono were reported at the time to be based in Moscow to prepare Communist propaganda for Malaya and Indonesia. The spread of Communism was noticeable among Malays in Kuala Pilah, Terengganu and Malacca, and Malay membership at the time of the Labour Union was estimated to be between 400 and 500.

Dalley reported, too, in May 1932, the formation of a Malay left-wing political party independent of Chinese influence, which Bassa was said to be organizing from Borneo (the name was not given). The following Malays and Indonesians, representing the States of Selangor, Pahang, Perak, Terengganu, and Singapore, were reported to be connected with it:

- Emed bin Abdul Hamid, a member of the PKI and a friend of Jamaluddin Tamin
- Abdul Rahman bin Barudin
- Mohamed Sa'ad bin Mansoor, a friend of Jamaluddin Tamin
- Sarjono, then First Secretary of PKI
- Senawi
- Zubir

Jamaluddin Tamin was arrested by the Singapore Special Branch on 13 September 1932. He was known to be a contemporary of Tan Malaka, Alimin and Moeso Soebakat, who had escaped after the 1926 revolt in Java, and had subsequently devoted his attention to the formation of the Partai Republique Indonesia, with its headquarters in Singapore. The members were recruited mainly from the overseas remnants of the PKI. When he was arrested, documents were found in his possession which helped identify him as Kaukita, the author of anti-British articles in the *Bintang Timor* (Eastern Star). Enquiries continued after his arrest resulted in the arrest of Tan Malaka in Hong Kong, where he was on his way from Shanghai to Bangkok "with funds and instructions".

According to Dalley, non-Chinese members of left-wing political parties in Singapore/Malaya consisted of some 30 Malay and Indian members of the "Communist youth movement proper", 1,000 Malay and Indian members of the Malayan General Labour Union, and 100 Malay and Indian members of the Peasants' Union. The development of nationalism and the awakening of political consciousness among the Malays was evidently growing, and it was thought likely that it would receive the support of the local Communist Party and political agitators of the Netherlands East Indies, who having fled their country after the 1926 revolt would still be in a position to carry out subversive activities from Malaya, which was the acclaimed policy of the Third International in the Nanyang.[19]

Malay Communist Party

Dalley commented, probably quite correctly, that a "Malay Communist Party" as such did not exist, although "sympathisers worked under Chinese heads of local Divisional Committees". He summed up the main difficulties for the formation of a Malay Communist Party as follows: religion, that is, the Islamic faith of Malays; lack of funds; the difficulties of the Chinese language; and Malay and Chinese cultural differences.

Nevertheless, in the Kuala Pilah district of Negri Sembilan, in 1932, the Special Branch disrupted what was referred to as a "communist organisation headed by local Malays", and in Lenggeng (Negri Sembilan), the Kaum Muda (Malay Youth Movement) was labelled "communist", simply because it was considered to be in advance of orthodox Islam. However, on balance, what was labelled "communist" was probably more nationalist than Communist. Nevertheless, wherever the Kaum Muda was strong, the fact remained that it was not opposed to Communist and left-wing propaganda of the PKI or Indonesian nationalism.

Instructional Letter from Central Committee of the China Communist Party to Malaya Central[20]

Dalley reported that in September 1933 an important letter from the "Central Committee of the Communist Party of China" to Malayan "Central" was intercepted, as copied below, which crystallized very clearly the aims of the Malayan Communist Party:

> We must realise that it is the proletarians and their allies — the peasants — who can carry out from beginning to end the anti-Imperialist movement and the agrarian revolution which, under the leadership of the proletariat and the Bolshevik Party, will in the end lead to the socialist revolution. In the progress of the anti-Imperialist campaign and the agrarian revolution, Malaya is a field for both. Due to geographic proximity, Malaya, as the vanguard of the colonial and semi-colonial revolution, has very intimate connection with China's revolutionary movement.... The party has so far done very little in this branch of activities and we must try our level best to overcome the defects....

We are of opinion that your party must be responsible for the question of organising a strong and united Malayan Communist Party in order to collect all different races and urge them on.

Undoubtedly, our party knows that the British Imperialists are very strong and that we are very weak. If we want to achieve immediately the success of our uprisings, it is more than impossible. The establishment of a Soviet Republic in Malaya will be closely connected with the revolutionary movement in China and India, but that it not to say that the consummation of the revolution in China and India must always be the antecedent of the Malayan Revolution, and you should not think that before the consummation of the revolution in China and India, the party activities in Malaya should be limited to exciting labourers and peasants to minor struggles. During this period we should make use of the chance to spread the influence of the Party, and whether we can do it successfully or not depends solely upon our decision as regards our future working schemes towards the path of revolution. It is by means of the daily struggles that we can unite the labour and peasant struggles against imperialism and for the racial independence movement. For this reason we must draw special attention to these struggles which will put us in a better position and earn us the confidence of the labour masses, as well as to the further development of the Communist Party, labour unions, and other mass organisations.

We must also know that the young labourers, peasants and some portion of the students will enhance the influence of the party in the midst of the revolutionary struggle. Consequently the development of the Communist Youth is also one of our important duties.

Activities of the Red Labour Union are also very important. The work should not be done by a few comrades only sent by us; you must train all your members to take part in it as a powerful organisation. We must act in such a manner that we will make the labour movement become an all-powerful movement in the making of struggles. Within the Labour Union, the Communist Party has to set up Communist Party and Communist Youth branches which must always be very active. To lead the work of the Labour Union, the Party has to pay special attention to absorbing into the Union female workers in factories and the rubber estates.

Organisations to oppose Imperialism are to be widely started in the names of 'Anti-Imperialist League', 'League of the Independence of the Malay Race', and 'League to support the Chinese Revolution'. There must be a central organisation to direct the activities, representative of the various races.

On the whole, 1933 was practically free from Malay and locally domiciled Indonesian "left-wing" activities, and it was admitted in February 1934 that the efforts of Malayan "Central" to graft upon the local Malay population an enthusiasm for the "Communism of Moscow" had not been successful. Even so, a nucleus existed of renegade Javanese and Sumatran revolutionaries domiciled in Malaya who could form the nucleus of a leadership of capable Muslims who could bring influence to bear along the lines of religion and nationalism whenever the opportunity occurred.

Around this time, MCP propaganda to Malays and Indians changed significantly from Chinese-inspired to the elementary presentation of Communist principles in readily understandable simple Malay with a minimum of Communist jargon and international political terms. In June 1935, a "Unification Committee" was formed by Malay Central composed of one Chinese, one Malay and one Indian for the purpose of unifying left-wing efforts in the three main ethnic groups.

As events in Indonesia unfolded — with Indonesians engaged in a bitter struggle against the return of the Dutch colonial power — MSS continued to monitor the situation. The MSS reported "careless talk" in coffee shops in the Malay kampongs, initiations into invulnerability cults, and the mobilization of underground cells of fighters in service of the "motherland".[21] In the neighbouring regions the religion card was also being played. In the predominately Malay region of Patani in southern Thailand, for example, following a military coup in November 1947 there was a shift to the right. Afraid of reprisal from the authoritarian Thai regime, local Malay leaders then launched a revolt. At one point more than a hundred Malay fighters sought refuge on the Thai-Malayan border, claiming that the Thai soldiers and police were rampaging in their villages and raping their women. Ties between the former Malay kingdom of Patani and the rest of Malaya go back a long way to when the former was a major centre of Islamic life. The possibility of Patani gaining its independence and separating from Thailand was certainly not lost on its Malay leaders, who sought the support of their co-religionists in Malaya to strengthen their cause.[22] Around the same time, in late 1947, the United Nations General Assembly passed a resolution calling for Palestine to be partitioned between Arabs and Jews, which perhaps gave the Patanis some hope that they could be partitioned off from Thailand.

The first Islamic political party in Malaya — the Hizbul Muslimin — was established shortly thereafter by Islamic religious leaders Ustaz Abu Bakar al-Baqir and Dr Burhanuddin Al Helmi.[23] Declaring that Islam promised a democracy with no class, race or national distinction, they agitated for immediate *Merdeka*, "the building of an Islamic society and the realisation of *Darul Islam*, an Islamic state".[24]

For many years, in fact, there had been friendly association with Indonesian political parties in Malaya. But none of these came to notice politically until just before the Pacific War, when Parindra, a fusion of Indonesian moderate political parties, including the old-established Boedi Oetomo, came to Special

Branch attention. Following the British re-occupation of Malaya after the Japanese surrender, several new associations of this kind were formed.

Early in November 1945, after the MSS had returned postwar to Singapore/Malaya, Abdul Ghani, an Indonesian born in Batavia who had lived in Malaya for many years and had worked for the Kempeitai, the Japanese secret police, during the Japanese Occupation, issued a manifesto to all Indonesians living in Singapore and Malaya. The manifesto stated that the Indonesian Labour Party would be inaugurated on 7 November 1945, and that all Indonesian workers should stop work on that day and, if possible, attend a meeting at the Communist-controlled General Labour Union (GLU). The newly formed Indonesian Labour Party later assumed the name Persatoen Kaoem Boeroh, which was abbreviated to Perkabis. The manifesto urged Malays to form a Malay National Party (MNP) throughout Malaya "to awake the national spirit of the Malays, fight for freedom of speech, press, assembly, religion, and support and sympathise with the independence movements in Indonesia, Indochina, Vietnam", and a large number of similar communist exhortations.

It was later determined that Abdul Ghani was employed by the General Labour Union to spread nationalist and Communist propaganda as the head of the GLU's Malay section to instil into susceptible Malays the Indonesian concept of "freedom". At the end of 1945, he drew attention to the national flag of Indonesia, which he pointed out was the flag of Hang Tuah of Melaka, the legendary Malay leader, flown over the former kingdom of Majapahit, which then included Indonesia and Malaya.

MSS reports suggested that Ustaz Abu Bakar and other left-wing Malay leaders predicted that a revolution would erupt in southern Thailand and that the uprising would spread to Malaya and bring the British to their knees. Rumour had it, too, that the

MCP was looking to support the Malay left-wing revolutionary cause to present a united front to overthrow British colonial rule in Malaya and Singapore, and to this end it made an effort to give its Malay sympathizers, such as Abdullah C.D. (Cik Dat Anjang Abdullah), Abu Samah Mohamad Kassim and Rashid Maidin, who became leaders of the MCP's Malay 10th Regiment then operating in the jungle in Pahang, important roles to play in its uprising, to counter the general misconception that there was racial discrimination in the MCP.[25]

Malayan Emergency

On 15 June 1948, Dalley reported in the *PIJ* that there had been nineteen cases of murder and attempted murder and three cases of arson during the first half of June.[26] There was further evidence that the MCP was behind the campaign and indications that it was mobilizing ex-MPAJA personnel and others for jungle operations. Only one or two men were to remain in open premises to maintain an "appearance" of business as usual. Labour contractors, particularly those known to support the Kuomintang, bore the brunt of the MCP attacks, which were made mainly in Perak and Johor, the states which appeared to have the strongest concentration of MCP personnel in them.

At this juncture, too, perhaps it would not be amiss to refer to Anthony Short's book on the Malayan Emergency which criticizes Dalley for not forecasting when the first Malayan Emergency would start. However, Dalley could hardly be blamed for this as it was most likely due, as Chin Peng said at the Australian National University (ANU) workshop held in Canberra on 22–23 February 2003 by the Centre of the Chinese Southern Diaspora, that he himself was not aware until after it had happened that some members of his CPM jungle army had "jumped the gun" on

12 June 1948 and murdered three British rubber estate managers in the Sungei Besi district of Perak, with the result that the colonial government declared a state of Emergency in advance of the timetable Chin Peng had in mind.[27]

On the propaganda side, the editor of the *Min Sheng Pau* (Voice of the People), which was the party organ of the MCP from 1 June 1949 onwards, was arrested and charged with sedition. A long list of thirty-three overseas addresses from the MCP's files was found in his possession. The *Vanguard Weekly*, which is the organ of the Communist Pan-Malayan Federation of Trade Unions, contained inflammatory material which suggested that "workers of Malaya should follow the example of their comrades in Vietnam", who are taking part in a war of emancipation against the French colonial power.

Meanwhile, in the Federation of Malaya, a revision of the Trade Unions Act enabled the Registrar of Trade Unions to close all State Federations of Trade Unions and the pan-Malayan Federation of Trade Unions. In Singapore, the Singapore Federation of Trade Unions, which did not fall under the ban, threatened to call a one-day strike, but it failed to materialize as it was considered that its hold on the waterfront was not yet strong enough for them to do so.

The probability of Indonesian and Malay participation in a campaign of terror was considered, and, if this came about, according to Dalley, the MNP, PETA, API, and the Peasants Union would line up with the MCP, while UMNO and its Youth Corps would support the government. In Indonesian circles in Malaya, rumours were prevalent that hostilities in Indonesia against the Dutch would break out again — there was a rebel force of "young Indonesian Republican Colonels" in Sumatra in favour of continuing hostilities against the Dutch — and Dalley recorded further efforts of the PKI to stir up trouble in Malaya and establish a branch in Malaya to obtain arms and ammunition for the Communist Party of Indonesia. This may not be as farfetched as it sounded, as Singapore in particular had long been used as a banking, trading and communication centre to instigate strikes and labour discontent just across the Causeway in Malaya by the Indonesian Republican movement, and, in fact, some of the rebel groups in Indonesia were believed to be backed by Chinese and Indonesian businessmen based in Singapore. These interests were normally restricted to ordinary commercial pursuits, but of late there had been indications that attempts had been made to purchase firearms and other military equipment which were readily available from WWII surplus material, mostly in the Philippines.

The compilation of these political events by Dalley is, therefore, of some importance to the political history of Singapore and Malaya in general, and intelligence history in particular, for it describes how leaders of radical Malay organizations such as the Hizbul Muslimin, the Malay Nationalist Party (MNP) or the Malay cadres of the MCP would from time to time appear on the same platforms and broadcast similar messages: "We are living in a democratic era in a world of revolution ... we are fighting to retain our human rights ... Our greatest enemies are the capitalists ... Let us be called Communists and so on. We are fighting for our lives".[28]

With the PKI making seemingly unrestricted incursions into Peninsular Malaya to agitate the Malay left-wing to fight the British as they were fighting the Dutch, for the reasons which have been adverted to previously, Dalley was determined to focus his attention on the developing political situation in Malaya.

At this stage, after reviewing the information provided by Dalley in his above reports, one can only but agree with his summing up when he commented, in order to follow the threads through this intricate pattern, it is necessary to follow the activities of individuals. Some names have already been mentioned and most of these names will be repeated. But there are many important names left unmentioned in this paper: to include them all would take up too much space and to those who are unacquainted with the names and their aliases it might be confusing. For that reason this paper will be confined as far as possible, to a brief history of events. In the same way there are many satellite organisations whose history and activities are very relevant to this subject, but to include a detailed history of them all would make this paper too long and cumbersome.[29]

Meanwhile, in Indonesia itself, while this was going on, the Dutch, who considered that the Indonesians had co-operated with the Japanese during the Japanese Occupation of Indonesia during the war, were preparing to return to Indonesia to restore their pre-war colony, the Netherlands East Indies. It will be remembered that the Japanese surrender to the Western (Allied) powers was followed by the Indonesian declaration of independence by Sukarno and Hatta on 17 August 1945, which certainly made the situation very difficult for the returning Dutch colonial power. Moreover, when a Brigade of the 23rd British Indian Infantry Division finally landed in Java in October, its main task was the repatriation of POWs and Dutch civilians held by the Japanese, and as far as possible to maintain the peace between the Republican Indonesians and the Dutch. The Dutch had to come to terms as best they could with the Republicans, and if possible iron out any differences before 30 November 1946 when the British wartime Southeast East Asia Command came to an end and British forces would be withdrawn from the area.

Notes

1. Material for this and the following chapter is based on the two Supplements that Dalley provided for the MSS *Political Intelligence Journal* nos. 10/47 and 11/48.
2. Tim Harper, "A Long View on the Great Asian War", in *Legacies of World War II in South and East Asia*, edited by David Koh Wee Hock (Singapore: Institute of Southeast Asian Studies, 2007), p. 7.
3. In the meantime they were successful in evacuating to Singapore large numbers of civilians, men, women and children on the first stages of their repatriation to Holland. The author, who was in Singapore at the time, remembers seeing large numbers of them being accommodated temporarily in the rooms and grounds of what was the old colonial Raffles Hotel.
4. *British Association of Malaya (BAM) Historical Collection*, BAM II/8, MSS Supplement to the *Political Intelligence Journal*, "Indonesian Influences in Malaya" (JD Dalley/MG), dated 30 June 1947.
5. Yong Mun Cheong, *The Indonesian Revolution and the Singapore Connection 1945–1949* (Leiden: KITLV Press, 2003), p. 191.
6. Governor General of the Dutch East Indies 1942–48.
7. Secret, J.D. Dalley, Supplement no. 5, "Malay and Indonesian Communists", MSS *Political Intelligence Journal* no. 11/48 dated 15 June 1948.
8. Professor Cheah Boon Kheng included Colonel Dalley's Supplement no. 5 issued with *Political Intelligence Journal* no. 11/48 as an appendix to his excellent study *From PKI to the Comintern, 1924–1941: The Apprenticeship of the Malayan Communist Party* (Ithaca: Southeast Asia Program, Cornell University, 1992), but he did not attribute it to Dalley, probably because the copy he used was taken from PRO file CO 537/3752, which does not show its authorship.
9. Secret, J.D. Dalley, Supplement no. 5, "Malay and Indonesian Communists", MSS *Political Intelligence Journal* no. 11/48 dated 15 June 1948.

10. A derogatory term often used in Singapore/Malaysia for southern Indians.
11. Secret, J.D. Dalley, Supplement no. 5, "Malay and Indonesian Communists", MSS *Political Intelligence Journal* no. 11/48 dated 15 June 1948, p. 3.
12. Ibid.
13. See "Hainanese as Malayan Communists", in *The Origins of Malayan Communism*, by C.F. Yong (Singapore: South Seas Society, 1997), pp. 69–78, 84–85.
14. Partai Komunis Indonesia (PKI) was an important political force in Indonesia throughout the mid-twentieth century. It is perhaps not generally realized that during its peak it was the third-largest Communist party in the world, only superseded in strength by the Russian and Chinese Communist parties. In Indonesia it was a legal political party operating in the Indonesian political system, although opposed to Dutch colonial rule, and active from 1929 until it was closed down in 1965.
15. The South Seas Communist Party, also called the Nanyang Communist Party, was established in 1925. "Nanyang" was the Chinese term for "Southeast Asia". It was disbanded in 1930 when the Malayan Communist Party (MCP) was formed.
16. See Joseph Ducroux in *The Origins of Malayan Communism*, by C.F. Yong (Singapore: South Seas Society, 1997), pp. xv, 99, 136, 155, 170, 274, 163–64.
17. A copy of the records of the former Shanghai Police files, including its Special Branch files, is held in the National University of Singapore Library.
18. Secret, J.D. Dalley, Supplement no. 5, "Malay and Indonesian Communists", MSS *Political Intelligence Journal* no. 11/48 dated 15 June 1948, pp. 14–17.
19. Ibid.
20. Ibid., pp. 14–15.
21. Christopher Bayly and Tim Harper, *Forgotten Wars: Freedom and Revolution in Southeast Asia* (Cambridge, MA: Harvard University Press, 2007), p. 417.

22. For more information on the Patani revolt, see Rohan Gunaratna and Arabinda Acharya, *The Terrorist Threat from Thailand: Jihad or Quest for Justice?* (Washington, DC: Potomac Books, 2013).
23. Ustaz Abu Bakar founded the religious institute, Madrasah Maahad Il Ihya Assharif, in Gunung Semanggul, Perak. Dr Burhanuddin was a schoolteacher in Singapore before WWII and in 1945 helped found the Malay Nationalist Party (MNP), successor to the left-wing Kesatuan Melayu Muda (KMM) in Perak. Burhanuddin wrote many protest letters to the press on what he referred to as the Israeli Occupation of Palestine, and was even arrested for protesting against it. See <https://www.malaysia-today.net/okay-now-my-version-of-history> (accessed 20 October 2017).
24. Bayly and Harper, *Forgotten Wars*, p. 418.
25. Deborah Loh, "The Voice of the Malay Communists", *The Nut Graph*, 4 December 2009 <http://www.thenutgraph.com/the-voice-of-the-malay-communists/> (accessed 20 October 2017).
26. Secret, J.D. Dalley, MSS *Political Intelligence Journal* no. 11/1948 dated 15 June 1948, p. 408.
27. See Anthony Short, *The Communist Insurrection in Malaya 1948–60* (London: Frederick Muller, 1975). Reprinted as *In Pursuit of Jungle Rats: The Communist Insurrection in Malaya* (Singapore: Cultured Lotus, 2000).
28. Bayly and Harper, *Forgotten Wars*, pp. 418–19.
29. Secret, J.D. Dalley (BAM 11/8), Supplement to MSS *Political Intelligence Journal* no. 10/47 dated 30 June 1947, p. 4.

Chapter 6

Indonesian Encroachment into Malaya

It was undoubtedly a difficult time for any intelligence service. As related previously, Dalley was faced with a serious problem in focusing his attention on the intrusion of PKI elements and supporting left-wing Indonesian political parties into Malaya with the intention of subverting the MNP, Kaum Muda, and other left-wing Malay political parties to rise up against British colonial rule in Malaya, just as the Indonesians had done against the Dutch in Indonesia after the Japanese surrender in August 1945.

Firstly, there was the proximity of Indonesia to Malaya, which was only a stone's throw away across the narrow Straits of Melaka. Medan in Sumatra is only an hour's flight from Penang in Malaya, and even in so-called "normal" times there had always been a considerable amount of illegal traffic, in junks and other small craft engaged in smuggling goods — as well as illegal immigrants — into Malaya from Indonesia, which was difficult to intercept.

In those immediate post war days, immigration control on the west coast of Malaya facing Indonesia became increasingly difficult to impose.[1] Many senior British immigration officers had been killed during the Japanese war or were medically boarded out after the war, and they had been replaced by less experienced Malay immigration officers who were not always adverse to their Muslim brothers being allowed to enter Malaya, especially as they spoke more or less the same language, followed the same religion, and looked the same, and not very much attention was given to whether they had valid immigration documents or not. It was probably not considered, anyway, they would create a problem by joining the large numbers of Indonesians who had already been living in Malaya for years.[2]

There was perhaps another more radical school of thought that Malaya should have declared independence from the British on 17 August 1945, just as the Indonesian nationalist leader Sukarno had done in proclaiming Indonesian independence from Dutch colonial rule at the time of the Japanese surrender, as it does not seem likely that the Japanese would have prevented them from doing so as they did not appear averse to leaving behind after their departure political problems for the returning Western colonial powers to settle.

During Dalley's time it should not be overlooked, too, that Singapore's present-day external Security and Intelligence Division (SID), responsible for gathering and analysing intelligence relating to the external security of Singapore, did not exist, and it was not established until several years after MSS was wound up. If it had existed, it would have made it much easier for Dalley to obtain reliable information about internal developments in Indonesia.[3]

There was much discussion, adverted to in previous chapters, of how MSS would likely be affected by the establishment of SIFE in 1946, that is, a branch of MI5 in Singapore with the backing of the Colonial Office in London, especially when it became apparent that SIFE would no doubt be considered more important than MSS when it became firmly embedded at Phoenix Park, a sort of

"Miniature Whitehall" in Singapore, which was the headquarters of Malcolm MacDonald, British Commissioner-General for South East Asia, after he moved his headquarters there from the Cathay Building.

As noted by the historian A.J. Stockwell:

> While in 1946-47 Governor Gent had taken seriously the Indonesian/Islamic threat, by early 1948 MacDonald and the Colonial Office were convinced that any danger that may once have been of the disruption of Malaya by Moslem fifth-columnists had now receded.... Instead of a threat, Indonesia was now seen by the British government to be a potentially crucial ally in Asia. By the end of 1948 the British in Malaya were fighting a war against Communism not Islam.[4]

Meanwhile, Dalley's task had been further complicated by the emergence of Western soldiers of fortune or adventurers joining in the Indonesian turmoil to make easy money on the black market by selling war-surplus military items — then readily available at the end of WWII in many parts of Southeast Asia — to the Republicans in their fight against the Dutch.

Some of these adventurers were involved, too, in smuggling opium from Indonesia into Singapore from stocks the Dutch had maintained there, which could be sold for huge profits to help the Republicans obtain funds to purchase military supplies, as well as pay the salaries of their diplomats and advisors. Even aircraft were available in those uncertain days, which could be flown in to Indonesia by former WWII U.S. Air Force pilots from as far away as the Philippines, provided there was money to pay for them.

However, there were some, but not many, foreign sympathizers who were genuinely interested in supporting the Republican struggle against Dutch colonial rule, and were not interested in making money out of it. Perhaps notable examples of these would be the British John Coast and the British-American Muriel Stewart Walker, who adopted the Balinese name of K'tut Tantri to show her affection for and identification with things Balinese and Indonesian and became an English-language news broadcaster for the Indonesian Republic.[5]

To divert somewhat, John Coast (1916–89) was a subaltern in the British Royal Norfolk Regiment who had been captured by the Japanese at the fall of Singapore on 15 February 1942 and sent to work on the infamous "Railroad of Death" in Thailand. It was there in Japanese POW camps that he first met Indonesian POWs and became interested in Indonesian culture and in learning the Indonesian language, which he put to good use after the war in working for the Indonesian Republicans in their fight for independence. Coast's story is entangled with the history of the Indonesian Republic and its revolution against Dutch colonial power, blockade-running, and meeting and working for President Sukarno and other senior Indonesian Republic officials, which he wrote about in his book *Recruit to Revolution: Adventure and Politics during the Indonesian Struggle for Independence.*[6]

His story became involved, too, with the MSS, who were watching him very closely, when he met around this time in Singapore Nigel Morris, the MSS Deputy Director. As Coast writes, Morris wanted to see him about what he referred to as "this wretched opium affair". He found Morris, in his own words, "to be a man in his mid-thirties with sandy hair, straight eyes, a ruddy complexion, and of medium build. He looked a police officer but might have been a stock-broker or a yeoman farmer." Coast said that he explained to Morris that he had been sent by the Indonesian Republican Dr Hatta to try to find out the truth about what, if anything, had been happening.

I told him that I wished to clear the Republican Government's name as I had already done in Bangkok, and I had already passed on Dr Hatta's 'No Sales' order [of opium] to Kota Tinggi [*sic*], and lastly, if there was any evidence of opium coming into Singapore from Indonesia, Morris could expect the full cooperation of the Republican Government.

'All right,' Morris replied, 'if you are really prepared to cooperate, I'll be glad to pool certain information. Then you can tell me what you propose to do about it.' I nodded.

'Right. Now in the first place there's absolutely no doubt that Indonesian opium has come into Singapore. I have locked up here a young chap, an Indonesian-born Chinese, who had a large sum of money which he has confessed came from the sale of opium. I have a long statement from him and also from six other Chinese. Furthermore, my evidence checks precisely with the evidence of the Dutch police in Batavia. Between the two of us we have a complete account of how the smuggling was managed.'

'Here', opening a file on the desk before him. 'Take a look at it. You can see one example. This deals with a cargo of opium that came by speedboat from East Java last March.' He pushed the file across to me and I found myself looking at photostatic and original documents and statements which seemed to prove exactly what he had said.

'That's all the evidence I propose to show you at the moment. It should be enough. But I suppose you know all about Mr Cobley and his operations, too; I can assure you that his plane is carrying opium that he knows, and we know, is being landed just outside Singapore for the purpose of bringing it ashore here. We haven't found any of this opium yet; but we shall do. And that will be bound to cause a big stir. Now, tell me, what you propose to do about all this.'

'Well', I replied, my brain spinning, 'this is something of a shock, I must admit, but I can promise you this will also be news to Dr Hatta. I can guarantee that when I tell him of this he will instruct Dr Utoyo to co-operate with you in every way. I will make out a full report and urge that the Republican Government put a quick stop to these irresponsibilities — and for good.'

'Fine. Then if you can really do that, what can I do to help your side? What I mean is this: this has already caused a lot of unpleasant publicity, and I don't see any point in further disturbing the political atmosphere of the negotiations in Java if we can help it. What, for instance, would the Republican Government consider to be the most damaging thing that could come out of all of this?'

I looked at Nigel Morris and decided to trust him. I said slowly: 'The last thing the Republican Government would want would be for any of their ministers' names to be dragged in in connection with all this. I am quite sure this is the work of irresponsible people only. Could you protect us in any way?'

Morris said: 'Yes. I think that's quite easy. We don't want to lay any blame on any particular individual. I'll certainly do my best.' We shook hands, and as I got to the door he called after me, 'Good luck to your press conference!'[7]

Meanwhile, Dalley was becoming concerned about his own position as it became increasingly clear MSS would not be allowed to continue in Singapore after SIFE had been established there. It will be remembered he was aware, too, that even Colonel W.N. Gray, the newly appointed Malayan Commissioner of Police, whose opinion had been sought, considered that the MSS should be abolished and that political and security intelligence matters should be taken over by the Special Branch as a department of the police.[8] Meanwhile, the efforts of Dalley's main supporters, Malcolm MacDonald and Gimson, the Singapore Governor, realizing that the very existence of MSS was threatened by SIFE, continued to support Dalley and the MSS and they tried their best to find alternative employment for him to ensure that his services as an experienced intelligence officer should not be lost to Singapore.[9]

MacDonald, after consulting General Sir Neil Ritchie, Commander-in-Chief, Far East Land Forces, Singapore, and Air Chief Marshal Hugh Pugh Lloyd, the senior RAF officer, suggested that a new appointment should be made for Dalley "in SIFE as Head of South East Asia Division", but Sillitoe replied that this clashed with other plans that he had made for Hugh Winterborn, one of his own officers, who eventually headed SIFE from 1947 to 1948. Sillitoe's views were that Dalley was "sensitive" about his status and, in any case, he felt that Dalley would prefer to retire on pension on abolition of office rather than accept a subordinate position in SIFE.

Malcolm MacDonald commented rather strongly in a minute he sent to his senior staff officer Sir Ralph Hone that "Sillitoe's effort to force on us proposals which he knows that we shall object to makes an extremely unpleasant impression on me and is calculated to destroy confidence between the Defence Co-ordination Committee, the High Commissioner in K.L., and the Governor of Singapore."[10]

MacDonald nevertheless persisted in making enquiries to see whether there would be any suitable position available for Dalley in the "Malayan Police or Political Intelligence" in Malaya to ensure that Dalley's long experience of security intelligence would not be lost to the country, but Alexander Newboult, the Malayan Chief Secretary, replied that, unfortunately, there were no such positions available.

It is abundantly clear from the records that every effort was made by Dalley's supporters to retain his services in an intelligence capacity but they failed, and Dalley was finally told that MSS would be wound up and on the abolition of his office he would be retired.

Dalley retired to the UK on pension with effect from 11 April 1949, and he left Singapore by air on 1 September 1948 after taking into account the accrued leave he had accumulated during his long service.[11]

The functions of MSS were taken over by the newly resuscitated Singapore and Malayan Police Special Branches, which marks the beginning of another chapter in the history of British intelligence in Singapore.

As I commented in my earlier book *Malaya's Secret Police 1945–60: The Role of the Special Branch in the Malayan Emergency*,[12] the official annual reports of the Malayan and Singapore police forces are silent as to the actual reasons for the demise of Dalley and the MSS, but the *Report of the Police Mission to Malaya* (1950), in referring to the winding-up of the MSS, concludes rather laconically that "it made for efficiency to distribute its [MSS] work and staff among the two Special Branches".[13] But the real reason is likely to be found in the government's perceived dissatisfaction with the performance of MSS as its main intelligence agency and its failure to warn the Malayan government in good time of the MCP's intentions to wage war on it, as well as the Colonial Office's tacit approval of MI5's intention to establish SIFE in Singapore and its reluctance to support MSS.

On reviewing the information available, there is no doubt, however, that Dalley's personality played a not inconsiderable part in the government's decision to dissolve the MSS. From what the author has heard from police officers who knew Dalley, he could at times be untactful and a rather difficult person to deal with, and he did not always endear himself to many of his former police colleagues when he made it clear that he regarded the MSS as his own separate "empire" outside the established police and intelligence structure. He has been described by several Special Branch officers who knew him as a "prima donna" and a "loner", who ran the MSS very much as his own "cloak and dagger" operation.[14]

As perhaps to be expected, in the view of Sillitoe's MI5, he was an "Empire builder, could not delegate responsibility and was convinced that he was the sole expert on intelligence in the Far East ... [and] the shortcomings of [the] Malayan Security Service seriously hampered the work of SIFE and the personality of Dalley thwarted any attempt to remedy the situation."[15]

In an extraordinary way, too, between 1946 and 1950, it is not generally realized that Sillitoe was making determined attempts in other parts of the world to expand MI5's influence to acquire many of the intelligence functions being performed by MI6, the UK's external intelligence organization under his opposite number Sir Stewart Menzies, which caused Menzies to comment at one time that it appeared that Sillitoe was planning to operate "a single world-wide secret service", although in the end the main differences between MI5 and MI6 were patched up between them over an amicable lunch at Menzie's London Club.[16]

The reversion of MSS to separate Special Branches in Singapore and Kuala Lumpur will be dealt with in the next chapter.

Notes

1. Secret, FCO 141/16880 P.R.O., The Secretariat, Government of the Malayan Union, Kuala Lumpur, to the Governor-General, Singapore, (14) in M.U. Union 497/C/47 dated 23 September 1947.

2. Secret, BAM II/8, MSS Supplement to *Political Intelligence Journal* no. 10 dated 30 June 1947.
3. Singapore's Security and Intelligence Division (SID) (Divisi Keselamatan dan Perisikan) is Singapore's external intelligence agency. It was established in February 1966 for gathering and analysing intelligence related to the external security of Singapore.
4. A.J. Stockwell, "Imperial Security and Moslem Militancy, with Special Reference to the Hertogh Riots in Singapore (December 1950)", *Journal of Southeast Asian Studies* 17, no. 2 (1986): 322–35.

    Stockwell's view may not be quite right, however. The official ongoing commission by Sir Lionel Leach into the Maria Hertogh riots in Singapore, which commenced on 11 December 1950, reports that Indonesians played a large part in the ferocious attacks on Europeans and Eurasians in Singapore. The Leach Commission Report opined that Indonesian feelings against the Dutch may have been transferred to the British whom they believed supported the Dutch Consul-General in the Hertogh case. See "Report of the Singapore Riots Enquiry Commission 1951, together with a Despatch from His Excellency the Governor of Singapore to the Rt. Hon. the Secretary of State for the Colonies" (Singapore Government Printers, 1951), p. 51.
5. Walker, Muriel Stewart (aka K'tut Tantri), *Revolt in Paradise* (London: Heinemann Asia, 1960).
6. John Coast, *Recruit to Revolution: Adventure and Politics during the Indonesian Struggle for Independence* (Copenhagen: NIAS Press, 2015).
7. It is ironical that Coast did not seem to realize that his own salary as a Republican advisor came from the sale of opium, or if he did, he kept quiet about it.
8. *British Association of Malaya Historical Collection*, Political and Constitutional, BAM III/8, "Twenty-Nine and a half Years in the Malayan Civil Service", H.P. Bryson, April 1963.
9. *Malcolm MacDonald Papers*, Durham University Library, box 16, MAC 16/02/1-58, file 2 of 2: South East Asia/Malaysia: Governor

General: "Colonel Dalley 1946-1948. Dalley's Employment; SIFE Appointments, Work of SIFE".
10. Malcolm MacDonald Papers, Durham University Library, microfilm records NAB 153 and NAB 23253 in Singapore Archives, undated handwritten memo from Malcolm MacDonald to Sir Ralph Hone.
11. See *Annual Report of the Singapore Police Force 1949*, p. 14. See also CSO (C) 10201/48 dated 17 March 1949 from the Colonial Secretary to the Officer Administering the Government of the Federation of Malaya, which indicated that Dalley was required to be retired under Section 6(b) of the Malayan Establishment as the result of the abolition of his office.
12. Leon Comber, *Malaya's Secret Police 1945–1960: The Role of the Special Branch in the Malayan Emergency* (Singapore: Institute of Southeast Asian Studies; Victoria: Monash University Press, 2008), p. 43.
13. *Report of the Police Mission to Malaya, March 1950* (Kuala Lumpur: Government Press, 1950), p. 11.
14. Letters to author from Norman Cleaveland and D.A. Weir dated 17 November 1992 and 5 May 1995, respectively.
15. See Christopher Andrew, *The Defence of the Realm: The Authorized History of MI5* (London: Penguin Books, 2010), p. 448.
16. See Keith Jeffery, *MI6: The History of the Secret Intelligence Service 1909–1949* (London: Bloomsbury, 2010), pp. 634–36.

Chapter 7

Arrangements for Allocation of MSS Staff to Special Branch, Singapore, and Special Branch, Malaya

The final details of the transfer of MSS officers and staff were decided at meetings held by the Commissioner of Police, Singapore, and the Colonial Secretary, Singapore, on 20 August 1948[1] and a meeting at the Singapore Special Branch on 25 August attended by A.J. Kellar, Head of SIFE; I.S. Wylie, Assistant Commissioner, Special Branch, Federation of Malaya; and N.G. Morris, Assistant Commissioner, Special Branch, Singapore, with E. Leighton, DSO (Defence Security Officer), Singapore and Federation of Malaya, in attendance.

It was agreed that the finances of the two Special Branches should be operated separately from 1 October 1948, and on that date the balance of the MSS funds would become available to the Singapore and Federation of Malaya Governments, respectively.

Officers Proposed for Transfer from MSS to Singapore Special Branch

Asst. Commissioner	N.G. Morris	Acting
Superintendent	A.E.G. Blades	Acting
Chinese Section	B.C. Fay	ASP
Indian Section	R.B. Corridon	ASP
Malay & Indonesian Section	H.J. Woolnough vice T.Q. Gaffikin proceeding to Federation of Malaya	ASP
General, Foreign & European & Other Section	A.R. McEwan	ASP
Registry	W.T. Knott	Archivist

It was proposed that Woolnough, then based in Johor, should head the Malay and Indonesian Section, as shown above. The **Assistant Commissioner** would be made in charge of administration and be responsible for the collection and collation of all political information affecting the security of Singapore. He would also be expected to maintain close contact with other intelligence organizations in Malaya and neighbouring countries.

The **Superintendent** would be employed mainly on Communist organizations and would coordinate and direct the activities of all sub-branches. In connection with Communist activities, he was required to pay frequent visits to the Federation of Malaya and contact officers there whom he might wish to consult.

The **General, Foreign and E & O Section** would be employed on general enquiries, including affairs of Europeans,

Eurasians, Siamese and foreign nationals not mentioned above, counterespionage, security of information in Singapore and surveillance.

Interrogations connected with the "Emergency Regulations" (which were introduced after the outbreak of the Malayan Emergency) would be carried out by F.G. Minns, ASP, "but as he is already on the Singapore CID staff, there is no extra expense involved in this post".

In addition to J.E. Fairbairn, who held the rank of Local Security Officer, MSS, but was not a member of the Police Force, there was, too, J.H. Ellen, who was a direct appointment to the MSS and was not a member of the Police Force. It was proposed that Ellen should be employed by the Special Branch, Federation of Malaya, and that Fairbairn should be offered an existing vacancy (due to the integration of the MSS and the Police establishment in the Singapore Police) as a Cadet ASP in the Singapore Special Branch, subject to any training required by the Singapore Commissioner of Police.

To accelerate the setting up of the Singapore Special Branch, it was proposed that the following acting appointments should be gazetted as soon as possible, pending recommendations for substantive appointments at a later date:

Acting Deputy Commissioner — E.V. Fowler
Acting Asst. Commissioner — N.G. Morris
Acting Superintendent — A.E.G. Blades

Archivists: J.F. Allen and W.T. Knott were then archivists at MSS HQ. It was decided that Knott should remain based in Singapore and Allen would eventually become available for service in the Federation of Malaya. As Allen was due to proceed on home leave on 17 September 1948 and Knott some six months later, this meant that for the next six months only one archivist would be available to the two governments. As there was still one month or so before Allen proceeded on leave, however, it was agreed that his services should meanwhile be made available to the Assistant Commissioner SB in Kuala Lumpur in the initial stages of building up the Kuala Lumpur registry.

Lady Confidential Secretaries: There were 8 lady confidential secretaries employed at MSS HQ and it was proposed that 4 of them should remain with the Singapore Special Branch. The rest were not transferable due to family obligations, but from 1 October 1948 financial provision was made available for the Kuala Lumpur Special Branch to employ locally 4 lady confidential secretaries.

Inspectors and Detectives: There were no inspectors or detectives on MSS HQ strength. However, Inspector Choo Ooi Chin and a detective corporal who had recently been attached to Singapore from the Federation of Malaya would be redeployed to the Federation of Malaya.

MSS Clerical and Miscellaneous Staff at MSS HQ consisted of 2 Malay writers, 1 financial assistant, 7 clerks and interpreters, 2 stenographers, 1 senior Chinese interpreter, 13 translators, 1 linotype operator, 1 linotype mechanic, 4 peons, 10 constables (orderlies) and 4 special constables (drivers), but none of these personnel would be transferable to Malaya for the following reasons:

(a) They had spent the whole of their service in Singapore and had no experience of the Federation of Malaya.
(b) They were Singapore Government servants, and though in some cases there was provision for service outside Singapore, this would not be enforced without the agreement of the staff concerned, and none of the clerical staff were agreeable to transferring to Kuala Lumpur.

Note

1. C.P. (Confidential), 90/S dated 20 August 1948, from Commissioner of Police, Singapore, to the Colonial Secretary, Singapore, "Reversion of MSS to Police Special Branch. Proposals for Setting up the Special Branch in Singapore in place of the existing MSS".

Chapter 8

Conclusion

Thus the MSS was wound up and separate Special Branches were once again established in Singapore and Kuala Lumpur reporting to their respective Commissioners of Police. However, to complete this account of Singapore and Malaya's domestic intelligence services, when Singapore merged a few years later with the Federation of Malaya on 16 September 1963 to become part of "Greater Malaysia" with Tunku Abdul Rahman as Prime Minister, the Singapore Special Branch soon realized that it now had to serve more than one master. It not only reported to its own Director and the Singapore Commissioner of Police but it was required to report as well to the Director, Special Branch, Kuala Lumpur, and the Inspector-General of the Royal Malaysian Police as part of Greater Malaysia.

Who can ever forget Singapore's Prime Minister Lee Kuan Yew shedding tears on TV when he announced what amounted to Singapore's expulsion on 9 August 1965 from Greater Malaysia by Tunku Abdul Rahman, as Malaysia began to look less favourably on the effect that would be felt by absorbing the large predominantly Chinese population of Singapore on the overall ethnic balance of the new Greater Malaysia.[1]

But the Singapore Special Branch of what had by then become the independent Republic of Singapore, soon consolidated its position and looking ahead to 17 February 1966 the Singapore Government converted the Special Branch into the Internal Security Department (ISD) which assumed responsibility for the country's domestic political and security intelligence. It was separate from the Singapore Police Force although working closely with it whenever required. This has remained the case until today, although the title "Special Branch" has been retained in Malaysia, where it is still a division of the police.

At the same time, the foundations of Singapore's external intelligence service were formed and the Security and Intelligence Division (SID) came into existence.

In fact, many Singapore Special Branch officers in those early days hardly noticed the change and continued to think of themselves as "Special Branch", but during the intervening years the ISD has established itself and become the formidable, impressive and much admired intelligence organization it is today.

To revert to Dalley and the MSS, after he retired, Dalley's services were recognized on 8 July 1949 by the award of the King's Police Medal, which is undoubtedly a highly prestigious police decoration.[2] But, nevertheless, to the end he still remains somewhat of a controversial figure, as many of the old-time senior Malaysian Police officers in the present-day Senior Police Officers Mess, Kuala Lumpur, still remember the criticisms which come up whenever his name is mentioned, whereas others feel that he should have been awarded a higher decoration for the distinguished services he rendered Malaya and Singapore as Commander of Dalforce during the war and for developing Singapore's intelligence service afterwards as Director of the MSS.[3]

In summing up, it is hoped that this preliminary study through the lens of the archives will be of use in presenting an overall account of Lieutenant Colonel John Dalley, of the development and demise of the little-known Malayan Security Service which he commanded, as well as the establishment of SIFE as a branch of MI5, the British intelligence service, in the Singapore/Malayan area.

Notes

1. Leon Comber, *Singapore Correspondent: Political Dispatches from Singapore (1958–1962)* (Singapore: Marshall Cavendish, 2012), p. 9.
2. See the *Straits Times*, 22 July 1949. The caption of the accompanying photograph reads: "Lord Listowel, Minister of State for Colonial Affairs presents the King's Police Medal to Lieut.-Colonel John Douglas Dalley, former Director of the Malayan Security Service, Lieut.-Col Dalley organised Dalforce in Singapore during the last war."
3. Author's notes.

Appendices

Appendix 1
Diagram of Communist & Left-Wing Malayan and Indonesian Political Movements

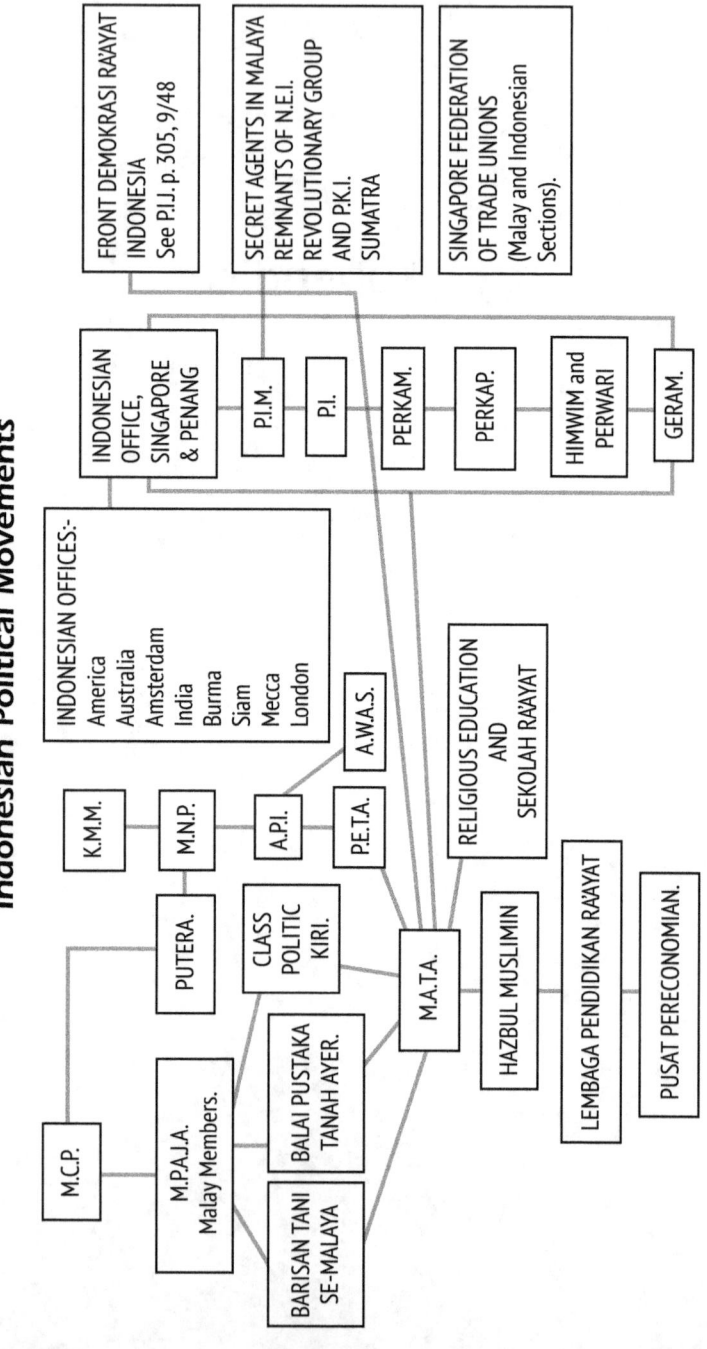

Key to Diagram

M.C.P.	Malayan Communist Party.
M.P.A.J.A	Malayan People's Anti-Japanese Army.
PUTERA	Pusat Tenaga Ra'ayat. (Malay Council of Joint Action).
BARISAN TANI SE-MALAYA	Peasants' Union, Malaya.
BALAI PUSTAKA TANAH AYER	Patriotic Publishing House.
CLASS POLITIC KIRI	Left-wing Political Class.
M.A.T.A.	Majlis Islam Tertinggi. (Supreme Islamic Council).
HAZBUL MUSLIMIN	Muslim Political Council.
LEMBAGA PENDIDIKAN RA'AYAT	People's Cultural Association.
PUSAT PERECONOMIAN	Economic Council.
K.M.M.	Kesatuan Melayu Muda. (Malay Youth Union).
M.N.P.	Malay Nationalist Party.
A.P.I.	Angkatan Pemuda Insaf. (Enlightened Youth League).
P.E.T.A.	Pembela Tanah Ayer. (Youth Defence Corps).
A.W.A.S.	Angkatan Wanita Sedar. (Assocn. Of Enlightened Women).
P.I.M.	Persatuan Indonesia Merdeka. (Indonesian Independ. Movement).
P.I.	Persatuan Indonesia. (Indonesian Association).
PERKAM	Perpaduan Ra'ayat Kalimantan. (Assocn. Of People of Borneo).
PERKAP	Persatuan Kurinchi Peranakan. (Kurinchi Association).
HIMWIM	Himpoenan Wanita Indonesia Malaya. (Indonesian Women's Welfare Assocn.)
PERWARI	Persatuan Wanita Republic Indonesia. (Indonesian Women's Association).
GERAM	Gerakan Angkatan Muda. (Youth Movement).
FRONT DEMOKRASI RA'AYAT INDONESIA	People's Democratic Front of Indonesia.

Source: Secret, J.D. Dalley, Supplement no. 5, "Malay and Indonesian Communists", MSS *Political Intelligence Journal* no. 11/48 dated 15 June 1948.

Appendix 2

Supplement no. 9 of 1948 issued with Malayan Security Service *Political Intelligence Journal* no. 14/48 dated 31 July 1948

> *This paper may have been Dalley's parting shot at MIS/SIFE before he departed from the political scene in Singapore to emphasize, as it were, that MIS/SIFE would not have been able to produce a report of this kind as it did not employ its own secret agents in Singapore/Malaya and had to rely for information on the local Special Branch.*
>
> *He may have issued it, too, to counter the allegation that was often made that he was too "Malay oriented" and did not pay sufficient attention to the Malayan-Chinese dominated MCP.*
>
> *Dalley's paper is not particularly elegantly written, has some omissions and appears to have been written in haste — perhaps for the reasons mentioned above. But it does nevertheless indicate his understanding of the MCP's aims.*

A REVIEW OF MALAYAN COMMUNIST PARTY POLICY.

Introduction [by MSS]

While the danger is still present and the smell of gunpowder is still in our nostrils it is important to look back and examine how this situation was permitted to arise in order that with determination equal to that with which the Emergency is now being tackled we may prevent a recurrence when the danger has receded.

The ensuing review of M.C.P. policy, supported by documentary evidence wherever possible, is submitted for this purpose together with landmarks of Government policy and other factors which may have had a bearing on the prolonged struggle between the two. (Some conclusions are given on the last page.)

MALAYAN COMMUNIST PARTY POLICY.

1. In 1943 the M.C.P announced a 9-point programme which included:-

> "(1) Drive out Japanese Fascists from Malaya and established [sic] a Malayan Republic.
>
> (5) Reorganise the Malayan People's Anti-Japanese Army into a regular army for national defence.
>
> (9) Unite with U.S.S.R. and China to uphold the independence of Far Eastern oppressed races."

2. In January 1945 the M.C.P. compiled "an analysis of the international situation and notes on the Malayan revolution" which contained the following passages:-

   i. The M.C.P. is the only political party which has all along been leading the revolution in Malaya.

   ii. All around Malaya are colonies in which revolutionary struggle against oppression and racial emancipation are being carried out by revolutionary organisations. They cannot achieve success unilaterally. Concerted action is necessary and there should be a common aim, unified policy and identical slogans.

   iii. Today (1945) the anti-Fascist Allies (Britain and the U.S.A.) are reliable. Their attack on the Japanese is positive but this cannot bring about a change in their capitalistic policy.... If the Malayan people want to achieve their complete emancipation they must be self-reliant, expand their own strength and be prepared for a more determined and a more bitter bloodshed struggle."

3. By August 27th 1945 the M.C.P. had deemed it wise to revise and reduce their previous policy from 9 points to 8 points, from which the following are those corresponding to the points quoted in Para. 1:-

> "(1) Support the democratic alliance of Soviet Russia, China, Britain and America. Support the new international peace organisation.
>
> (8) Treat the anti-Japanese armies kindly and help the families of the fallen warriors."

Note: With regard to point (8) above, information obtained in June 1948 shows that the M.P.A.J.A. ex-Service Association were planning a large scale swindle to obtain demobilization gratuities for non-existent personnel, the money to go to the M.C.P. and not to members of the M.P.A.J.A. or their families.

4. In August or September 1945 the leaders of the M.C.P., then under WRIGHT alias LOI TEK (萊特) [Lai Teck] were said to have been offered the use of Japanese troops and arms to fight against the incoming Allied forces. WRIGHT refused this offer.

5. In September 1945, immediately after the liberation, the M.C.P. organised movements to mobilize the forces of labour, youth and women.

6. October 10th 1945 was one of the first days of celebration after the liberation and LIM AH LIANG (林亞亮) of the Singapore Town Committee of the M.C.P. commemorated this Double Tenth with an article in the Chinese press from which the following is a quotation:-

> "We should not forget that it is through Soviet Russian leadership and sympathy for the weak and small nations and

the oppressed masses that China's successful war of national liberation and the Allied victory over world Fascism have been made possible."

7. On October 25th 1945 the inauguration ceremony was celebrated in Singapore of the General Labour Union, forerunner of the Singapore Federation of Trade Unions, and the Pan-Malayan Federation of Trade Unions. The organisers were pre-war leaders of the underground Red Labour Union now in 1945 free to operate unhindered.

[MCP Manifesto on Current Situation]

8. On November 7th 1945 the anniversary of the Soviet Revolution was commemorated by the M.C.P. with the issue of a manifesto on the current situation and coloured printed posters calling upon the people to follow the lead of the Soviet. A brief summary translation of the main portion of the M.C.P. manifesto is as follows:-

This printed booklet entitled "M.C.P MANIFESTO ON CURRENT SITUATION" dated 7th November 1945, published by the Central Executive Committee of Malayan Communist Party and addressed to the dear brethren of all races in Malaya extols the remarkable achievements of the Communist Party of U.S.S.R. in abolishing the capitalist system and emancipating the Russians from poverty and servitude and then establishing in their stead a democratic Soviet Russia in which peasants, workers and the intelligentsia now all live in equality, freedom and happiness. It says that Soviet Russia is the champion for world peace and world security. It advocates the abolition of race oppression and the unreasonable social system of exploitation of men by fellow beings. It traces the historical facts from 1935–1939 showing how the U.S.S.R. worked incessantly for a united front against the Fascist challenge but was betrayed by capitalist powers with the Munich intrigue plunging the world into a great catastrophe, but thanks to the immense strength of the Red forces the anti-Fascist war was brought to a victorious end." "But, however", the manifesto points out, "this success is temporary and the danger of war still exists for the following reasons:

1) Reactionary elements in many countries are still actively trying to revive the old form of domination to oppose democratic rule.

2) Reactionary elements are still trying to keep the small and weak nations in Eastern Europe and the Balkans in the hands of the puppets of the Capitalist Class, controlled by the Powers, but denying them their right of self-determination.

3) The British, Dutch and French Imperialists are bent on maintaining their system of colonial Government in Malaya, Indo-China and Indonesia."

[Demobilization of MPAJA, 1 December 1945]

9. On December 1st 1945 the M.P.A.J.A. handed in arms and was officially demobilised. The return of arms was claimed to be highly satisfactory but in spite of this it is now believed that the M.P.A.J.A. retained a secret army of over 4,000 men and that they may have retained a large number of arms previously reported as unaccounted for after parachute drops. The demobilised open army at once formed M.P.A.J.A. ex-Service Associations in all important districts, thus maintaining their organisation in being.

10. On December 9th 1945 the inauguration ceremony was celebrated of the New Democratic Youth League [N.D.Y.L.] representing the culmination of the M.C.P.'s efforts to reorganise the pre-war Communist Youth League.

11. In January 1946 the Party held its 8th Central Extended meeting at which WRIGHT was re-elected with universal acclaim as Secretary-General to the Party in spite of the circulation of accusations that he had betrayed the Party to the Japanese. In an article on the "present short-comings of the Party" it was agreed that the Party had not shown sufficient initiative in leading the masses and had relied too much upon the opportunist policy of following up behind the natural reactions of the people freed from the Japanese yoke.

12. In January 1946 a working plan for the unification of all Malaya was drawn up by the Central Executive Council describing the chief lines of policy in the labour and youth movements and for propaganda work. It is recorded in this plan that the "N.D.Y.L. should be regarded as an advanced political body of youths and as a first step Communist Youth Corps. The N.D.Y.L. should come within the jurisdiction of the Communist Youth Organisation".

Under propaganda, a list of anniversaries is given including the "15th February - Fall of Malaya". Although not mentioned in the document it is known that the Communists wished to celebrate this day as marking the date from which they took over control of Malaya from the defeated British in 1942.

With regard to labour an interesting warning is given in this plan as follows:- "Beware of the possibility of the British Imperialists importing labour into Malaya from Siam and other places as this will affect the establishment of Party strong-points in industry and the sponsoring of labour movements".

13. On January 29th 1946 the M.C.P. through G.L.U.s [General Labour Unions] tested its strength with a general strike which lasted for two days. It was regarded as a sweeping success by the M.C.P. The B.M.A. refrained from taking action under the Trade Dispute Ordinance against the organisers for calling an illegal strike.

[MSS Opinion of MCP]

14. On February 14th 1946 the situation had deteriorated to such an extent that the B.M.A. was obliged, if it was to continue to exist, to take action against the Singapore Town Committee of the M.C.P. for publication of seditious articles in the press defying the Administration's ban on processions and assemblies in celebration of February 15th in the manner referred to in paragraph 12. Ten Communist labour leaders or propagandists were arrested and subsequently banished. LIM AH LIANG (林亞亮), leader of the Singapore Town Committee, was arrested on the following day for obstructing the police and taking out a procession illegally and was subsequently convicted for rioting and also on two counts of sedition. It is known that it was WRIGHT himself who called off more widespread extremist operations at the last moment. This action by the B.M.A. had a very sobering effect on the activities of the M.C.P. but it was pointed out at the time in a memorandum dated February 19th 1946 that

"it is our (M.S.S.) opinion and the opinion of the majority of the Chinese population that if the present Communist Party is permitted to continue to exist as a legal society, it will become impossible for the British Government to maintain control and we may as well stop trying to do so now. Even though drastic action is taken for a short period and everyone detained is expelled from the country, the same dangerous situation will soon arise again if the Communist Party is not declared illegal. We compare the Communist Party to a fruit tree which is rotten. No matter how many times the fruits are plucked, all are bad, and it would be much better to cut down the tree."

In spite of this the Supreme Allied Commander showed the greatest reluctance to issue expulsion orders for the ten leaders arrested and he left the matter over to be decided as the very first act of the Civil Government on its resumption of authority on April 1st 1946.

[Outline for Malayan People's United Front]

15. On March 1st 1946 the M.C.P. issued a booklet entitled "An Outline for the Malayan People's United Front". This contained the following passage:-

"Based on the situation strategy of the Comintern, the strategy of the M.C.P. is to conduct and consummate a democratic revolution – which is to say an anti-Imperialist and a 'landed property' revolution – in order to build up a nation after the Soviet pattern with an absolutely democratic government of the industrial and rural masses, which is the prerequisite for a social revolution. Such indeed is the ultimate objective of the Malayan democratic revolution."

It also contained plans for co-operation on an opportunist basis with the Malayan Democratic Union, the Malay Nationalist Party and with capitalists for specific objects of mutual advantage.

[1 May 1946 Labour Day Rallies]

16. On May 1st 1946 the first monster Labour Day rallies were

held throughout the country and they demonstrated the capable organising capacity of the Party and an attitude of defiance towards any authority not imposed by their own officials. The Party appeared to have recovered completely from the set-back received in February 1946.

17. June 22nd 1946 was celebrated by the Party as the anniversary of the outbreak of war between Soviet Russia and Germany and the Soviet was again extolled as "the star of salvation of the weaker races of the world".

18. In July 1946 the Central Executive Committee issued a review of the current international and Malayan situation from which the following are extracts:

"The duplicity of American foreign policy in Europe and China, aided and abetted by British reactionaries, is interpreted as an anti-Soviet, anti-Communist and anti-Democracy move on the part of the capitalist bloc."

"Since the political development of Malaya is closely related to British Imperial policy, which is anti-Soviet and anti-Communist, political reform as advocated at the present moment is only meant as a temporary measure to dampen the fighting spirit of the people, gain time and place on firm ground colonial rule."

[Missing Sections in Dalley's report]

...exemption or registration. The M.C.P. in common with the K.M.T. [Kuomintang], C.D.L. and other political organisations staged a protest against the re-introduction of this Ordinance which they deemed to be an infringement of free political rights. At the last moment the Government sought means of extricating itself from this awkward situation and amended the Ordinance to permit the Governor in Council to grant exclusion from the provisions of the Ordinance to established political organisations amongst which the M.C.P. and its satellites, the M.P.A.J.A ex-Service Association, the N.D.Y.L. and the Women's Federation were accepted.

[Wu Tian Wang Propaganda Tour]

27. On June 17th 1947 WU TIAN WANG (伍天旺) returned from the United Kingdom and proceeded on a propaganda tour of Malaya. It is known that he was disappointed with the lukewarm reaction of the British Communist Party towards M.C.P. affairs. One tangible result of the conference was the distribution by the M.C.P. of newsletters to a number of Empire Communist Parties, but they have received very little in response. WU TIAN WANG (伍天旺) is believed to have been appointed a correspondent of the *Daily Worker* and also to have been given free cable facilities to the left-wing press agency Telepress, but has made little or no use of either of these facilities.

28. In June or early July 1947 the M.C.P. held its 9th Central Extended Conference at which a further plan was adopted to unite the masses (details are not available).

[Iron Discipline of MCP 1947]

29. In June 1947 the M.C.P. issued "The Iron Discipline of the M.C.P. 1947". This contains details of the probationary period for qualification as a member of the Party which varies from 3 months in the case of the working class to 9 months or possibly

15 months in the case of the better educated. The following quotation from a chapter on "Obedience" is of interest:-

"Organisations of the lower stratum shall be obedient to organisations of the upper stratum in carrying out resolutely all resolutions and instructions received from the latter. At the same time, the organisations of the upper stratum shall have power, if deemed necessary, to dissolve or reconstitute organisations of the lower stratum. This is a method by which it is possible to maintain unanimity in the Party. Otherwise, there will be several groups in the Party, and there will be no central orders and no concerted actions."

30. In July 1947 the Selangor State Committee issued a booklet showing that in the past 18 months the strength of the Party in that State had steadily decreased and that only 27% of the Party members in the State were installed in Trade Unions. 29 members had been expelled or had left the Party.

[All Malaya Council of Joint Action, July 1947]

31. In July 1947 the M.C.P. issued policy instructions on support for the All Malaya Council of Joint Action from which the following are quotations:-

> 1) The Party should support the Council of Joint Action, a propertied class set-up, at its initial stage of unity and induce it to take part in the Party-organised struggles, so that the democratic elements of which it is composed may improve and advance themselves. It is the aim of the Party to make this propertied class democratic movement become a branch of the people's democratic movement.

2) The Party, in its endeavour to bring the propertied class to align itself with the people's united front, should modify its own slogans and draw up a programme to be based on the needs of the propertied class as well as those of the labourers and peasants.

3) The Party should strive to win the respect and recognition of the propertied class for itself and for the labour and peasant forces. The Party would stand a better chance of attaining and maintaining a legal status if it were respected and its services appreciated by the propertied class. The Party must not allow itself to become the "tail" of the democratic movement, but it should have its own slogans and programme of activities and it should also create a solid mass force, having the innumerable labourers and peasants as its backbone. The Party should also support the propertied class democratic movement and help it to intensify struggles.

4) The Party should not be content with the announcement of anti-feudalist (anti-Sultans) slogans. It should exploit the conflict between the people's united front and the feudalist force, and artfully bring it to a climax at an early date. It should also employ the combined forces of the people, the Malay force in particular (note:- the M.N.P. are commonly referred to with XXs), to undermine the power and influence of the feudalists in the cause of anti-imperialist struggles.

5) The Party should show its respect for the Malay race by giving them concessions in its programme. The Party's Malay members who are participating in

XX (M.N.P.) activities should conceal their political identity and resort to secret techniques so as to avoid misunderstanding on the part of XX, which might think the Party is trying to manipulate its organisation and to gain control of its lower strata. Whatever proposals or requests for co-ordination of efforts the various State or District Party organisations may put before XX, they should relate to problems of the Malay race so that the Malay section will not be led to think that the Party is making use of the Malay force to support Chinese activities and also to further their interests."

A warning was issued also about the weakness of the A.M.C.J.A.

[World Federation of Democratic Youth Convention, Prague]

32. On July 4th 1947 CHEN TIAN (陳田) and LEE SOONG (李送) were sent by air to attend the World Federation of Democratic Youth Convention at Prague. They are known to have met Soviet officials in Paris. It is stated by the Perak prisoner, whose interrogation report has already been quoted, that there were three objects of this visit to Europe:-

(a) To find out if WRIGHT had escaped to Europe.

(b) To investigate his claims to international Comintern status in Europe.

(c) To discover what support could be expected from Communists in Europe for a revolt in Malaya.

The same source reports that these two were successful in exposing WRIGHT's false claims but did not bring back any promise of support for the M.C.P. owing to distance. CHEN TIAN was said to have been particularly disappointed with the British Communist Party which had tendencies towards the Right and was not extreme enough.

33. On August 10th 1947 the A.M.C.J.A. / PUTERA Group announced agreement upon the adoption of their so-called People's Constitution. The Singapore M.C.P. representative issued a statement that the Party would support the People's Constitution although it did not go as far as the Party would wish.

34. On August 16th 1947 LIM AH LIANG, Singapore M.C.P. leader, was released from prison and given a riotous welcome by the M.C.P. Although he was a more important leader than the ten men banished in April 1946, although convictions for criminal offences had been recorded against him and although there was not a single dissenting voice on the Advisory Council when his banishment was put up for consideration the Singapore Government decided that he would be regarded primarily as a political prisoner and that banishment action would be contrary to the spirit of instructions received from the Secretary of State.

35. On August 22nd 1947 the M.C.P. made much propaganda out of the funeral of an Indian coolie who was shot by the police in the Singapore Harbour Board while resisting lawful police action. An unruly and truculent procession was formed which adopted an anti-white and anti-police attitude.

36. On August 27th 1947 the M.C.P. went one better still on the occasion of the funeral of LIM AH LIANG who had died from natural causes on the previous day. Government were openly accused of being responsible for his death and many speeches and statements with a seditious tendency were made. An even larger and more unruly procession was taken through the town

and several excesses committed. The Party was at the peak of its exuberance during the period from August 16th to 27th in marked contrast to its deflation after the action taken by the B.M.A. in February 1946 when LIM AH LIANG had been the ring leader. Such a complete reversal could not but be expected to breed an air of over-confidence in the M.C.P. and of bewilderment among the public at the apparent weakness of the Government.

37. On September 16th 1947 the C.E.C. issued a policy direction on how to make use of the strength of the Chinese Chamber of Commerce in the anti-Constitution campaign. A warning is given that the People's Constitution, the objective of the A.M.C.J.A. / PUTERA Group, must be kept firmly in view and the people must not be allowed blindly to follow the Chinese capitalists to any other goal. This was a piece of pure opportunism always strongly suspected and now confirmed.

38. On October 20th 1947 occurred the combined Hartal, the one occasion when even K.M.T. members of Chinese Chambers of Commerce were aligned with the M.C.P. against Government.

39. On November 20th 1947 CHEN TIAN and LEE SOONG returned from Europe.

40. In December 1947 the committee on WRIGHT reported results and it was decided to expel him from the Party. It was decided to announce this gradually step by step down the Party.

41. From the beginning of the year rumours of a third world war, which had been referred to as early as November 7th 1945 (see Para. 8 above), began noticeably to increase in intensity. It is thought that these rumours were deliberately spread as a part of M.C.P. propaganda policy.

[Chou En Lai's Advice, 1948]

42. In January or February 1948, the Perak Communist under interrogation states, the M.C.P. sent a messenger to Hongkong to seek China Communist Party advice from CHOU EN LAI (周恩來) upon a revolt in Malaya. The latter is said to have replied that in a colony bloodshed was the only means of achieving a Communist revolution.

43. On February 1st 1948 the new Federation Constitution was introduced without much ado except in Singapore where the Communist-controlled S.F.T.U. decided, independent of instructions from the All-Malaya C.J.A., to call a one-day strike which did not cause very great inconvenience as February 1st was a Sunday.

44. On February 2nd 1948 LEE SOONG left by air to attend the South East Asia Youth Conference at Calcutta.

45. On February 15th 1948 the Pan-Malayan F.T.U. held a meeting in Singapore in celebration of its second anniversary. The Singapore M.C.P. representative CHANG MIN CHING (張明今) spoke and reminded his audience not to forget that February 15th was a day of vengeance and sorrow for the Malayan people as well as the day on which the P.M.F.T.U. was inaugurated. He went on to say that:-

> "Bloodshed marked the inauguration of the P.M.F.T.U. two years ago. At that time the British Government made use of tanks and machine guns to suppress the people. Such action only increased the indignation and unity of the people. The British Government also made every attempt to undermine the Trade Union Movement."

[Lance Sharkey, Australian Communist Party]

46. On February 22nd 1948 L. SHARKEY, leader of the Australian Communist Party, passed through on his way to the Indian Communist Party Conference in Calcutta on February 26th.

47. On February 25th 1948 it is believed, from a secret source, that Dr. PHAM NGOC TACH, VIETNAM Communist leader, desired TAN PENG (陳平) alias CHEN PIN (陳平) M.C.P. leader, to attend a meeting in Bangkok.

48. From March 9th to 20th L. SHARKEY was in Singapore in transit for Australia after attending the Indian Communist Party Conference.

49. On March 16th 1948 the M.C.P. Central Executive Committee issued instructions to State Committees upon how labour should be organised to resist police action in labour disputes and cause sabotage.

[MCP Central Executive Committee 4th Plenary Conference, March 1948]

50. From March 17th to March 21st 1948 the M.C.P. Central Executive Committee held its 4th Plenary Conference. Full details are not known but the following are extracts from a resolution entitled: "Existing Situation" which was passed at this Conference:

"A fundamental change has taken place in the postwar International situation. As a result of her winning the war against Fascist aggressors, U.S.S.R. has emerged as a determining factor and enabled the democratic influence of the people adhering to socialism to occupy a transcendent position in the postwar world arena. This is made possible by the military defeats suffered by the Fascist bloc, by the diminution during the war of the strength of Imperialism, thereby laying bare the emaciated condition of her capitalism after the war."

"The serious split in the policies of these two camps (Imperialist and anti-Imperialist) has rendered it no longer possible for the world Powers to come to a compromise to co-operate. Instead, national, political, economic, ideological and sectional military struggles are spreading and tending daily to assume serious proportions. Confronted with such serious struggles some are inclined to ask: "Is there a possibility of another world war breaking out?" Whilst it is true that Imperialism now is putting more efforts into preparation for war than before, it is equally true that the strength of the peoples throughout the world for checking a war of aggression is greater now than ever before. Therefore, a distinction must be drawn between the theoretical efforts and aspirations of the Imperialists, which drive them to plan for war, and the practical possibility of their being able to organise for such a war. This is because it is one question whether they are thinking of fighting or not, and quite another whether they are "able to fight or not. This, however, is not to say that as a natural consequence war will never come because we must recognise the fact that as long as Imperialism exists, so long will the danger of war remain. Therefore, it is neither right to become panicky and lose one's self-confidence upon hearing about the danger of war, nor is it right to adopt a carefree, complacent attitude and so relax one's vigilance in the face of preparations for war on the part of the Imperialists."

"Therefore, the danger facing the anti-Imperialist struggle of the labouring class and the people today lies in their underestimating their own strength while over-rating the strength of the Imperialist camp. It must be clearly understood that in the world situation today, the leading power does not lie with Imperialism but with the peoples throughout the world. The dominant position is not occupied by Imperialism but by Socialism. The strength of the world anti-Imperialist democratic camp far transcends that of the Imperialist anti-democratic camp. While Imperialism is daily weakening and fading away through a series of crises, Socialism and the world democratic strength are marching on unchallenged. By reason of the fact that the colonial peoples are the direct objective of exploitation of the Imperialists, the emancipation struggles in colonies have become an important and inseparable component part of the anti-Imperialist struggles of the peoples throughout the world. There are several points in the postwar policy of the Imperialists in suppressing the national emancipation movement in colonies viz:

[Colonial Suppression of National Emancipation Movement]

1) Resorting to military intervention and to armed attacks, hoping thereby to undermine the young Republics.

2) Setting up "independent nations" that actually do not enjoy any real independence, or enforcing "federal systems", hoping thereby to pacify the struggle spirit of the people and to break the unity of the people.

3) Carrying out the policy of "divide and rule".

4) Assisting in the growth of the feudalistic influence and the bourgeoisie, with a view to making them the running dogs of the Imperialists, and helping them to set up puppet governments, so as to divert the attention of the people from the real object of their struggle, and so combine to launch an attack on the people.

"All this, however, does not indicate that the foundation of the colonial rule of the Imperialists is becoming more stable, but shows in fact that that foundation is becoming more and more shaky in the face of strong resistance put up by the colonial people. The attacks launched by the Imperialists, coupled with the existence of some vacillating and traitorous upper stratum elements within the colonies, have given rise to new difficulties in the way of the emancipation movements in colonies, but the war has altered considerably the position in colonies, for the peoples have all awakened, and are resolutely pursuing the road to struggle. The wave of national emancipation is rising incessantly and the peoples in colonies are ceaselessly launching their counter-attack on the Imperialists. Under these circumstances, it is imperative that a new method must be adopted for the colonial people's struggle. This is by establishing a united front with the lower stratum workers and peasants as its foundation, by abandoning and delivering a blow to those few renegades of the upper stratum and by a widespread rallying of the masses, by means of practical action, to defeat Imperialist policy and to strive for complete independence and emancipation. And under the many phases of the situation, an <u>armed struggle</u> (i.e. the people's revolutionary war) is inevitable. For this reason, <u>armed struggle</u> bears a particularly important significance. In the struggles of the broad masses of the people within Imperialistic countries themselves and in their colonies, the world Communists are shouldering the most glorious task in history. It is clear that today only the Marxist Party – the Communist Party – is able to resolutely lead the masses to proceed with the anti-Imperialist struggle, to shoulder the task and responsibility involved, and to continue the struggle until complete victory is achieved. The peoples of the world are certain to support the leadership of the Communist Party, and unite within its fold."

"Although after the war, the British Imperialists have brought into effect certain improvements, yet it is not because of their sign-board of socialism, nor is it a gift from them, but because pressure has been brought to bear on them by the people. But such improvements are only preparatory measures by which to launch their attack in a devious way. Therefore, it is wrong to repose any hope in the British Parliament, in the Labour Party government and in her 'improvement' tactics."

"The conflict between the British Imperialists and the people is manifested in two phases: firstly economically, because of the intensification of exploitation of the British Imperialists, causing thereby a daily increasing suffering and hardship of the people, to which it is most imperative that we should start to take countermeasures, and secondly politically, because the British Imperialists are gradually wresting from the people whatever little democratic freedom they have, thereby creating widespread dissatisfaction among the people. It is imperative that we must struggle to strive for the basic human rights. These two phases of conflict continue to spread, and are becoming more and more acute daily.

In the course of this struggle, a change has taken place which indicates the weakening of the British Imperialists and the growth in that of the people, for the former has more and more to rely solely on their machineries of government to maintain their rule, while the latter, having been greatly disillusioned, being dissatisfied with, and even harbouring hatred for the British Imperialists and being greatly awakened, are continually increasing in their strength.

The demands or object of the struggle of the masses (more especially the labouring class) today though they principally involve the improvement of livelihood, do not stop short at that. The maniacal policy of the British Imperialists has changed the masses today from what they were before. They demand struggles everywhere and are not afraid of the attack of the British Imperialists. The masses realise that holding talks or negotiations are useless. What they must do is engage in a united and determined struggle.

Economically, the bourgeoisie in Malaya are of a vassal-like character, while politically they are either vacillating or tending to be opportunist. Therefore there is little possibility of their opposing the British Imperialists today. The strength of the struggle of the masses must essentially depend on the lower-stratum workers and peasants for its foundation.

This Party has had a long revolutionary history in Malaya. The masses know that this Party is one that renders service to the people, and is in the front line in maintaining the struggle. The struggle of the masses today needs the direction of this Party to lead them on with determination until victory is achieved."

[Lee Song Returns from Calcutta, 22 March 1948]

51. On March 22nd 1948 LEE SONG returned from Calcutta via Burma where he had been in touch with the Burma Peasant Organisation.

52. On March 26th 1948 D. PUHALO, W.F.D.Y. delegate to the Calcutta Conference, arrived from Rangoon, where he had been inciting the peasants to resist Government, and addressed a meeting of the N.D.Y.L. in Singapore. He was detained and expelled within 24 hours.

53. During the first week in April the rubber workers in several factories in Singapore showed signs of organised and truculent

resistance to lawful police action after their factories had been closed down and they had been given legal dismissal terms.

54. From April 5th to 12th the P.M.F.T.U. held its annual conference in Singapore at which it was made quite clear that the policy thenceforth was to be complete self-reliance and disregard for official mediation. All the regular Communist leaders of the P.M.F.T.U. were re-elected to office.

55. On April 8th and 9th 1948 the following entries were recorded in a diary belonging to the North Johore guerrilla leader TAN KAN (陳幹) who was killed in action on July 8th:-

"April 8th 1948. The month of May is the time of struggle. It is the time when the oppressed revolt against the evil spirits and executioners, fighting a bloody battle. The great month of May I look forward to you."

"April 9th 1948. Returned to Kluang today and making preparations to take part in the ... meeting. This is a very important meeting, it is the turning point of our work. Our policy, since the time of the anti-Japanese campaign, has been a wrong one. We seem to have fallen and surrendered into the doctrine of the rightists. Now is the time to wind up affairs. Human beings are born to struggle. It is hard to live in a Colonial Empire. To yield to hateful favours and to endure will not do any good, it is death. The way out is to stand united and to fight."

[Singapore Harbour Labour Union, 10 April 1948]

56. On April 10th the Singapore Harbour Labour Union issued seditious pamphlets from which the following is an extract:-

"Our strength of struggle cannot be overshadowed (sic) by the plotting, deceit and cunning measures of the British Imperialists. During the last 2 years odd the British Imperialists with their armed police have frustrated our strikes, culminating in 5 shooting incidents in which altogether 3 fellow labourers were killed. Several of those supervisors who maintained "order" during strikes were arrested and beaten and furthermore supervisor ANG KAH SENG (洪加成) is about to be banished by the British Imperialists.... All our fellow workers must settle these dripping drops of blood debt with the British Imperialists. We have already contracted with the British Imperialists such an enmity that both parties can no longer exist under the same sky. We have already got rid of our illusions about the British Imperialists and we are confident of our strength. All difficulties can be fundamentally solved only by the strength of our unity. If the employers continue to be obstinate and ignore the labourers' strength by being stubbornly reactionary to the end, we will start a sanguinary struggle against the British Imperialists with more intensity and on a larger scale."

[MPAJA Security Instructions, 15 April 1948]

57. On April 14th police action was taken against the S.H.L.U. and several arrests were made.

58. On April 15th 1948 the M.P.A.J.A. issued security instructions regarding documents, photographs, passes, etc. (Agent B.2).

59. On April 17th 1948 until the end of the month the S.F.T.U. did their utmost to maintain a strike in the Singapore Harbour Board and on several occasions hand-grenades were thrown and other acts of violence committed. In spite of this the strike was

unsuccessful, partly due to K.M.T. intervention but more, it is thought, to a fall in the labour market.

[MCP New Line Policy, April 1948]

60. On or before April 20th 1948 an article appearing over the name of CHENG CHIEH (鄭傑), a member of the Central Executive Committee of the M.C.P., was published in Chinese. This article contains indications of the adoption of a new line of policy by the M.C.P. The following is a quotation:-

"Until recently our Party had committed very serious mistakes in the course of struggles. Such mistakes originated from our Party's political line which, as pursued until recently, was one of rightist opportunism. It was manifested by our Party's abandonment of the programme for national liberation immediately after the war. Under the influence of such an opportunist line our Party was hoping against hope that Britain might reform her policy in Malaya and this in turn resulted in the unconditional yielding of our Party in the face of the British Government's reactionary offensives.... Under the influence of such an opportunist line our Party also committed certain mistakes in the course of "supporting the Constitutional struggle. We gave our support to the People's Constitution although its basic contents were incorrect. Its basic viewpoint was one of wistfully hoping that Imperialism might automatically reform its policy. Another mistake that we committed in connection with the Constitutional campaign was the mechanical separation of the top level activities among the various political bodies from the mass movement."

61. On April 23rd 1948 the S.F.T.U. staged a one-day strike in protest against search of their premises in connection with the offence of sedition committed by the S.H.L.U.

62. On April 24 and 25th 1948 the A.M.C.J.A./PUTERA held a conference in Singapore at which it was agreed that $4000 out

of the anti-Constitution fighting fund totalling $8000 should be given to the S.F.T.U. to aid persons on strike. Resolutions were adopted to fight against "the Red bogey campaign". TAN CHENG LOCK (陳禎祿) was eased out of his position as Chairman of the A.M.C.J.A.

63. On April 28th the S.F.T.U. defiantly challenged the decision of the Colonial Secretary that no procession should be allowed on May Day. This challenge was withdrawn on the following day after the Government had in return cancelled permission for a May Day assembly which had previously been granted.

[Labour Day, 1 May 1948]

64. On May 1st 1948 Labour Day was celebrated very quietly in the Federation and not at all in public in Singapore. The Singapore M.C.P. representative issued a statement from which the following is an extract:-

"Reactionaries are not strong and are no cause for fear. They are handicapped by numerous difficulties and weaknesses.

Being more weakened after the war, they have already lost their prestige. The Malayan democratic forces which won a victory over the Japanese Fascists will not withdraw in the face of intimidation.

If we fail to realise our own strength, become frightened or disheartened, or should we yield or compromise and depend on mediation and arbitration, our fate will be inevitable.

We do not want bloodshed but the authorities want us to shed our blood. We want tranquillity in Malaya but the authorities have created chaos."

The M.C.P. representative also said that under a financially weakened Imperialist British Government there was absolutely no hope of rehabilitation in Malaya.

65. On May 5th 1948 the M.P.A.J.A. held an executive council meeting in Kuala Lumpur. (Details not available).

66. By May 15th 1948 there were signs of mobilization of armed mobile corps in the Federation.

[Expulsion of Wright (alias Lai Tek)]

67. On May 28th 1948 the C.E.C. issued a pamphlet explaining the reasons for the expulsion of WRIGHT alias LOI TEK from the Party. This included the following extracts regarding policy:-

"After peace was declared, the policy fixed by him was essentially a 'running dog' policy, traitorous to the cause of the revolution. It can be clearly seen that he had been in league with the Imperialists to sabotage the revolution."

"Comrades of Central have endeavoured their utmost in getting the Party to turn away from a blind alley to a new path as evidenced by the recent fixing of a new policy which has gained the full and unanimous support of comrades of the entire Party."

68. At last on July 23rd 1948, when the house had been burning for over two months and the fire could no longer be disregarded, the Secretary of State consented to the proscription of the M.C.P. and its satellites in the Federation of Malaya and Singapore.

[MSS Conclusions of Review, 31 July 1948]

Conclusions drawn by M.S.S. from this review are as follows:-

1) M.C.P. policy was completely dominated by the traitor WRIGHT both before and after the liberation and his

prestige was so great that although he had run away in March 1947 it was not until December 1947 that the leaders of the Party considered that they had sufficiently convincing proof to be able to face the lower levels with the news of his exposure.

2) The opportunist policy adopted by WRIGHT continued after his departure until the end of 1947 when the extremists in the Party began to adopt a new line as they gradually became assured that they had survived the news of the expulsion of WRIGHT.

3) It is probable that the final decision to adopt a policy of violence was made at the C.E.C. meeting held in March 1948. The first stage was a stiffening on the labour front resulting in widespread labour agitation, particularly in Singapore and Johore during April. The second stage, of open armed revolt, was by April 9th already being looked forward to by the Johore leader, TAN KAN, for the month of May but the firm action taken by the Singapore Government in April may have affected their plans.

4) While it is obvious that external factors have influenced the change in M.C.P. policy since January 1948, in the absence of any definite evidence on this point no more can be said than that, at a minimum, external circumstances may have raised hopes, if they did not actually bring instructions, but that the immediate cause of the change could have been developments entirely internal, namely, reaction to WRIGHT's treachery, lack of progress, and frustration over alleged British restrictions, particularly the policy towards Trade

Unions. Since 1943 the M.C.P. has been endeavouring to build up an organisation through which they could bring about an armed revolt against the Governments of Malaya. There have been numerous indications that it was their intention to bring about such a revolt sooner or later and once they had completed their period of consolidation and eradicated the influence of WRIGHT the stage was set. Events in Europe and events in neighbouring countries would indicate that the time was set by external influences.

5) On the question of prevention it is only possible to say that internal measures, free from hampering external considerations such as effect on world opinions at a period when delicate international negotiations were taking place, could have lessened the magnitude of the Emergency if the Governments had tackled it in their own good time but there have always in any case existed conditions for an inevitable clash. As to prevention of a recurrence, until the people as a whole have shown themselves able to withstand organised intimidation by recourse to law there is no alternative but to ban any organisation, trade union or political party which is even suspected of using intimidation, as the M.C.P. has done, as a means of progress.

MALAYAN SECURITY SERVICE
31st July 1948
Singapore.

Bibliography

COLONIAL OFFICE RECORDS
National University of Singapore

CO 537   Colonies. General Supplementary.
              Original Correspondence (1759–1955).
CO825   Eastern Department. Original Correspondence (1927–46).
CO 1022   South East Asia Department.
              Original Correspondence (1951–53).
KV 4/423   Organisation and Functions of Security Intelligence Far East (SIFE). Top Secret.
FCO 141   Records of the Foreign and Commonwealth Office and Predecessors.
              Singapore: Pan Malayan Security Service; Security Intelligence Far East (SIFE), 1946.

REPORTS AND PRIVATE PAPERS
ISD Heritage Centre, Singapore; National Archives, Singapore; Arkib Negara, Malaysia; Canberra National Archives, Australia

Annual Report of the Singapore Police Force 1946. Singapore: Government Printer, 1947.

Annual Report of the Singapore Police Force 1949. Singapore: Government Printer, 1950.

British Association of Malaya (BAM) Historical Collection. Royal Commonwealth Library (RCL), Cambridge University, United Kingdom, 1947–65.

British Military Administration (Malaya) Papers. 1945–46.
Colonial Office List. London: HM Stationery Office, 1957.
Dato Sri C.C. Too Papers. Kuala Lumpur: University of Malaya Library.
FARELF (Far East Land Forces) Reports.
J.D. Dalley Papers. Oxford, Rhodes House Library, United Kingdom.
Malayan Establishment Staff List 1948. Singapore: Government Records.
Malayan Monthly Chinese/Malay/Tamil Press Summaries.
Malayan Monthly Political Reports from Federation of Malaya.
Malayan Security Service *Political Intelligence Journal*, 1946–48.
Malayan Weekly Situation Telegrams.
Malayan Weekly Police Summaries.
Malcolm MacDonald Papers. Durham University Library, United Kingdom.
Monthly Chinese Affairs Reports.
Monthly Political Reports from Singapore.
Supplement to London Gazette, 1946. London: HM Stationery Office, 1947.

NEWSPAPERS

Straits Times (Singapore), 1946–48, 2017.
The Times (London), 1951.

PERSONAL CORRESPONDENCE AND INTERVIEW

Correspondence with Guy Charles Madoc (former Head of the Malayan Special Branch and subsequently Director of Intelligence, Malaya), 1994–95.
Correspondence with Kenneth Foo (Asst. Director, Ministry of Home Affairs, Singapore), 2016–17.
Interview with Francis Stuart, Canberra, 28 January 1993.

BOOKS

Abraham, Colin. *"Their Finest Hour": The Malaysian MCP Peace Accord in Perspective.* Petaling Jaya: SIRD, 2006.
Andrew, Christopher. *The Defence of the Realm: The Authorised History of MI5.* London: Penguin Books, 2010.

Bibliography

Ban Kah Choon. *Absent History: The Untold Story of Special Branch Operations in Singapore 1915–1942*. Singapore: SNP Media Asia, 2001.

Bayly, Christopher, and Tim Harper. *Forgotten Wars: Freedom and Revolution in Southeast Asia*. Cambridge, MA: Harvard University Press, 2007.

Blake, Christopher. *A View from Within: The Last Years of British Rule in South-East Asia*. Somerset: Mendip, 1990.

Blythe, W.L. *The Impact of Chinese Secret Societies in Malaya: A Historical Study*. London: Oxford University Press, 1969.

Cheah Boon Kheng. *From PKI to the Comintern, 1924–1941: The Apprenticeship of the Malayan Communist Party*. Ithaca: Cornell University Southeast Asia Program, 1992.

Cleaveland, Norman. *Bang! Bang! in Ampang: Dredging Tin in Malaya's Emergency*. San Pedro: Symecon, 1973.

Coast, John. *Recruit to Revolution: Adventure and Politics in Indonesia*. London: Christophers, 1952.

———. *Recruit to Revolution: Adventure and Political Struggle during the Indonesian Struggle for Independence*. Copenhagen: NIAS, 2015.

Comber, Leon. *Malaya's Secret Police 1945–1960: The Role of the Special Branch in the Malayan Emergency*. Singapore: Institute of Southeast Asian Studies/Monash University Press, 2008.

———. *Singapore Correspondent: Political Dispatches from Singapore, 1958–62*. Singapore: Marshall Cavendish, 2012.

———. *Singapore Chronicles: Japanese Occupation*. Singapore: Institute of Policy Studies, National University of Singapore/Straits Times Press, 2017.

Corfield, Justin, and Michael Thomson, eds. *The Corian 1998*. Corio, Victoria: Geelong Grammar School, 1999.

Elphick, Peter. *Far Eastern File: The Intelligence War in the Far East, 1930–1945*. London: Hodder and Stoughton, 1997.

Gilberg, Trond, ed. *Coalition Strategies of Marxist Parties*. Durham, NC: Duke University Press, 1989.

Gunaratna, Rohan, and Arabinda Acharya. *The Terrorist Threat from Thailand: Jihad or Quest for Justice?* Virginia: Potomac Books, 2013.

Internal Security Department. *Reflections: ISD at Robinson Road and Phoenix Park*. Singapore: Ministry of Home Affairs, 2008.

———. *The ISD Heritage Centre — A Decade of Security Education, 2002–2012*. Singapore: Ministry of Home Affairs, 2012.

Jeffery, Keith. *MI6: The History of the Secret Intelligence Service, 1909–1949*. London: Bloomsbury, 2010.

Khoo Kay Kim, ed. *The History of South-East, South and East Asia: Essays and Documents*. Kuala Lumpur: Oxford University Press, 1977.

Lee Su Yin. *Rock Solid. The Corporate Career of Tan Chin Tuan*. Singapore: Landmark Books, 2006.

———. *British Policy and the Chinese in Singapore, 1939 to 1955: The Public Service Career of Tan Chin Tuan*. Singapore: Talisman, 2011.

Mahani Musa. *Kongsi Gelap Melayu di Negri-Negri Utara Pantai Barat Semenanjung Tanah Melayu 1821–1940-an* [Malay secret societies in the northern Malay States 1821–1940's]. Malaysia: MBRAS, 2003.

Modder, Ralph. *The Passionate Islanders — Singapore at War, 1941–42*. Singapore: Horizon Books, 2010.

Mohd Reduan Haji Aslie and Mohd Radzuan Haji Ibrahim. *Polis di- Raja Malaysia: Sejarah, Peranan dan Cabaran* [The Royal Malaysian Police: History, role and challenge]. Kuala Lumpur: Kumpulan Karangraf, 1984.

Morais, J. Victor, ed. *Who's Who Malaysia 1963*. Kuala Lumpur: Solai, 1964.

Murfett, Malcolm H., John N. Miksic, Brian P. Farrell, and Chiang Ming Shun. *Between Two Oceans: A Military History of Singapore from 1275–1971*, 2nd ed. Singapore: Marshall Cavendish, 2011.

Percival, A.E. *The War in Malaya*. New Delhi: Sagar, 1971.

Sanger, Clyde. *Malcolm MacDonald: Bringing an End to Empire*. Montreal and Kingston: McGill-Queen's University Press, 1995.

Sheppard, Mubin. *Taman Budiman: Memoirs of an Unorthodox Civil Servant*. Kuala Lumpur: Heinemann Educational Books (Asia), 1979.

Short, Anthony. *The Communist Insurrection in Malaya, 1948–60*. London: Frederick Muller, 1975. Reprinted as *In Pursuit of Mountain Rats: The Communist Insurrection in Malaya*. Singapore: Cultured Lotus, 2000.

Stewart, Brian. *Smashing Terrorism in the Malayan Emergency: The Vital Contribution of the Police*. Kuala Lumpur: Pelanduk (M), 2004.

Stuart, Francis. *Toward Coming of Age: A Foreign Service Odyssey*. Brisbane: Centre for the Study of Australian–Asian Relations, Griffith University, 1989.

Tan Y.L., Kevin. *Marshall of Singapore: A Biography*. Singapore: Institute of Southeast Asian Studies, 2008.

Walker, Muriel Stewart (aka K'tut Tantri). *Revolt in Paradise*. London: Heinemann Asia, 1960.

Wynne, Mervyn Llewelyn. *Triad and Tabut: A Study of the Origin and Diffusion of Chinese and Mohamedan Secret Societies in the Malay Peninsula, AD 1800–1935*. Singapore: Government Printing Office, 1941.

Yong, C.F. *The Origins of Malayan Communism*. Singapore: South Seas Society, 1997.

Yong Mun Cheong. *The Indonesian Revolution and the Singapore Connection, 1945–49*. Leiden: KITLV, 2003.

ARTICLES

Arditti, Roger, and Philip H.J. Davies. "Rethinking the Rise and Fall of the Malayan Security Service 1946–48". *Journal of Imperial and Commonwealth History* 43, no. 2 (2014): 292–316.

Blackburn, Kevin, and Daniel Chew Ju Ern. "Dalforce at the Fall of Singapore in 1942: An Overseas Chinese Heroic Legend". *Journal of Chinese Overseas* 1, no. 2 (2005): 233–59.

Comber, Leon. "The Malayan Security Service (1945–1948)". *Intelligence and National Security* 18, no. 3 (Autumn 2003): 128–53.

———. "Traitor of all Traitors — Secret Agent *Extraordinaire*: Lai Teck, Secretary-General, Communist Party of Malaya (1939–1947)". *Journal of the Malayan Branch Royal Asiatic Society* 83, no. 2 (299) (December 2010): 1–29.

Fossati, Diego, and Eve Warburton. "Indonesia's Political Parties and Minorities". ISEAS *Perspective* 2018, no. 37 (9 July 2018).

Hughes-Mullock, Robert. "White Ribbon, White Flag: The Life & Times of Captain G.F.A. Mulock DSO, RN". *Review Journal of the Naval Historical Collectors & Research Association* 19, no. 2 (2006).

Leirissa, Richard Z. "Transient and Enduring Legacies of World War II: The Case of Indonesia". In *Legacies of World War II in South and East Asia*, edited by David Koh Wee Hock, pp. 36–46. Singapore: Institute of Southeast Asian Studies, 2007.

Shaw, Alexander Nicholas. "MI5 and the Cold War in South-East Asia: Examining the Performance of Security Intelligence Far East (SIFE),

1946–1963". *Intelligence and National Security* 32, no. 6 (2017): 797–816.

Stockwell, A.J. "Imperial Security and Moslem Militancy, with Special Reference to the Hertogh Riots in Singapore (December 1950)". *Journal of Southeast Asian Studies* 17, no. 2 (1986): 322–35.

Yong Mun Cheong. "Indonesian Influence on the Development of Malay Nationalism, 1922–38". *Journal of the Historical Society* (July 1970): 1–11.

THESES AND ACADEMIC EXERCISE

Arditti, Roger Christopher. "Our Achilles Heel" — Interagency Intelligence during the Malayan Emergency. PhD dissertation, Brunel Centre for Intelligence and Security Studies, 2015.

Chew Ju Ern, Daniel. "Reassessing the Overseas Chinese Legend of Dalforce at the Fall of Singapore". Academic exercise for BA (Hons.) History, Singapore: National Institute of Education, Nanyang Technological University, Singapore, 2005.

Coe, John Josiah. "Beautiful Flowers and Poisonous Weeds. Problems of Historicism, Ethics and Internal Antagonism: The Case of the MCP". PhD dissertation (restricted), University of Queensland, 1993.

WEBSITES

Bennet, Darryl. "Bowden, Vivian Gordon (1884–1942)". In *Australian Dictionary of Biography*, vol. 13. Canberra: National Centre of Biography, Australian National University, 1993. Available at <http://adb.anu.edu.au/biography/bowden-vivian-gordon-9552> (accessed 29 January 2017).

"Communist Party of Indonesia". *Wikipedia* <https://en.wikipedia.org/wiki/Communist_Party_of_Indonesia> (accessed 20 October 2017).

"Second Supplement to the London Gazette of Friday, the 20th of February, 1948", no. 38218, 26 February 1948. Section 1: Pre-War Preparations/Operational Efficiency of Units in Malaya. Britain at War <http://www.britain-at-war.org.uk/WW2/London_Gazette/Malaya_and_Netherlands_East_Indies/html/operational_efficiency_of_unit.htm> (accessed 28 October 2002).

The Learning Network. "U.N. Partitions Palestine, Allowing for Creation of Israel (Nov 29, 1947)". *The Learning Network*, 29 November 2011 <https://learning.blogs.nytimes.com/2011/11/29/nov-29-1947-united-nations-partitions-palestine-allowing-for-creation-of-israel/> (accessed 20 October 2017).

"Location Scouting in British Newsreels Made before the Japanese Occupation of Singapore (1938–42)". *The Hunter: Location Scouting in Singapore's Filmic History* (blog) <https://sgfilmhunter.wordpress.com/tag/newsreel/> (accessed 16 October 2017).

Loh, Deborah. "The Voice of the Malay Communists". *The Nut Graph*, 4 Dec 2009 <http://www.thenutgraph.com/the-voice-of-the-malay-communists> (accessed 20 October 2017).

MT Webmaster. "Okay, Now My Version of History" (Updated with BM and Chinese Translation). *Malaysia Today*, 28 January 2010 <https://www.malaysia-today.net/okay-now-my-version-of-history> (accessed 20 October 2017).

Index

Note: Page numbers followed by "n" denote endnotes.

A
Abdul Ghaffar bin Abdul Rahman, 64
Abdul Ghani, 80
Abdullah C.D., 81
Abdul Rashid bin Maidin, 49, 61, 81
Abraham, Colin, 47
Abu Samah Mohamad Kassim, 81
Adat Perpateh, 67–68
Aliens, Central Registry of, Singapore, 5, 40
Alimin, Mas, 61, 68–69, 70, 74, 75
Allen, J.F., 101–2
All Malaya Council of Joint Action (AMCJA), 120, 122, 123, 124, 134–35
AMCJA. *See* All Malaya Council of Joint Action (AMCJA)
Andrew, Christopher, 41, 43n5
Ang Kah Seng, 133
Annual Report of the Singapore Police (1946), 14, 29n1

ANU. *See* Australian National University (ANU)
"atomic hot war", 45–46
Arditti, Roger, x
Australian Army deserters, 24
Australian Communist Party, 62–63, 126
Australian National Archives, ix
Australian National University (ANU), 81
Australian Security Intelligence Service, 42

B
Balan, R.G., 49
Barry, J.C., 14–15
Bendera Merah Society, 16
Bintang Timor, 75
Blades, Alan E.G., 6, 7, 11n11, 15
Blake, Christopher, 42, 44n10
Blythe, Wilfred L., 11n10
BMA. *See* British Military Administration of Malaya (BMA)

Bowden, Vivian Gordon, 25
British colonialism, 14, 46, 47, 56, 81, 88
British Communist Party, 49, 119
British Military Administration of Malaya (BMA), 13–14, 40, 116, 124
Browder, Earle, 68
Bryson, Hugh, 23–24
Bukit Serene, 27, 52
Burhanuddin Al Helmi, 79

C
CCP. See Chinese Communist Party (CCP)
CDL. See China Democratic League
Central Committee of Communist Party of China, 62–63, 76–81, 124, 136–37
Malayan Communist Party and, 49
revolutionary movement in, 77
Chen Pin, 126
Chen Tian, 122–23
Cheng Chieh, 134
China Democratic League (CDL), 118
Chinese Chamber of Commerce, 124
Chinese Communist Party (CCP), 48
Chinese Hainanese community, 69

Chin Peng, 50, 81, 82
Choo Ooi Chin, 102
Chou En Lai, 125
CID. See Criminal Investigation Department (CID)
Cleaveland, Norman, 17, 31n10
Coast, John, 91, 97n7
Cold War, 45
Colonial Office, London, 13, 27–28, 35–37, 40–41, 89–90, 95
Comber, Leon, 30n3, 43n7, 54n9, 98n12, 106n1
"Communism in Malaya" conference, 59
Communist guerrillas, 21–22
Communist Insurrection in Malaya, 1948–60, The (Short), 15
Communist Pan-Malayan Federation of Trade Unions, 82
Communist Party of Indonesia. See Partai Komunis Indonesia (PKI)
Corridon, Richard, 6, 10n7
Corry, Charles, 25
Criminal Investigation Department (CID), 3, 15, 16–17

D
Daily Worker, 119
Dalforce, 1, 19–24, 32n16
ammunition, 23

Index

demobilization allowance, 23
training school for, 22
Dalley, John Douglas, 1
   in Criminal Investigation
     Department, 16–19
   detractors, 8, 9
   family life, 7–8
   in Japanese POW camp,
     25–26
   and Malay secret societies,
     15–16
Dalley, Peter John Layard, 8
Davies, Philip H.J., x
Defence of the Realm: The
   Authorised History of MI5,
   The (Andrew), 41
Dickinson, A.H., 2–3, 9n2, 41
Dixon, C.E., 36, 37, 39, 41
Ducroux, Joseph, 71–73
Dutch colonial rule, 57, 72, 90

E
Ellen, J.H., 101
Elphinstone, W., 6
Emergency Regulations, 49, 52, 101
Empress of Asia, RMS, 23

F
Fairbairn, J.E., 6, 101
Federation of Malaya, 82, 100, 101, 104
First Malayan Emergency (1948–60), 7, 17, 29, 47, 52, 81

French secret service, x, 50, 71
Foh Toh Cheng, 20

G
Gavin, J.M.L., 17
General Labour Union (GLU), 73, 80, 116
Gent, Edward, 27, 47–49, 51–52, 55n10, 90
Gimson, Franklin, 42
GLU. *See* General Labour Union (GLU)
Gray, W. Nicol, 27, 28, 34n25, 93
Greater Malaysia, 104

H
Haji Mahmud bin Hashim, 71
Hall, C.W.D., 28
Han Chinese secret society members, 24
Hang Tuah, 80
Hatta, Mohammad, 57, 70, 84, 91–93
Herbert, Christopher Albert, 39
Hill, H.L., 25
Hizbul Muslimin, 79, 83
HMS *Sultan*, 25
"Ho Ming Lie", 69
Hone, Ralph, 40, 43n5, 94
Hung League, 24

I
Ibrahim bin Haji Ya'acob, 60

Ikatan Pemudah Tanah Ayer (New Democratic Youth League), 49
Indian New Democratic Youth League, 49
Indo-Chinese Communist Parties, 62–63
Indonesia, 46, 47, 58, 90
   Federation of Indonesian Trade Unions, 62
   independence, 57, 89
   left-wing parties, 46, 48, 56, 59–62, 88
   Muslims, 47
   opium smuggling, 90, 92
   "police action" in, 58–59
   revolution against Dutch, 91
   Union of Indonesian Seamen, 61–62
Indonesian Communist Party. *See* Partai Komunis Indonesia (PKI)
Indonesian encroachment into Malaya, 95–96
   Coast, John, 91
   Hatta, Mohammad, 91–93
   immigration control, 88–89
   MacDonald, Malcolm, 94
Indonesian Republican forces, 57, 58
Indonesian Revolution and the Singapore Connection, 1945–1949, The (Yong Mun Cheong), 58

Indonesia Youth Corps (Pemoeda Rahasia Indonesia), 57
intelligence and national security, 2–4, 8, 27, 35–39
Internal Security Department (ISD), vii–xi, xiii, 105
"Iron Discipline of MCP", 119
ISD. *See* Internal Security Department (ISD)
Ishak bin Haji Mohamed, 60
Izvestia, 62

J
Jamaluddin Tamin bin Maiden, 61
Japanese Communist Parties, 62–63
Japanese Occupation (1942–45), 13, 24, 28, 47, 80, 84
Javanese Communist Parties, 62–63, 64, 72
Johnson, Malcolm, 39
"Jungle Ambush Patrols" report, 17

K
Kellar, Alex J., 39, 99
Kempeitai, 50, 60, 80
Kesatuan Melayu Muda (KMM), 27, 60–61
Khaw Kai Boh, 50, 54n9
Kirke, C.M.J., 6, 7
KMM. *See* Kesatuan Melayu Muda (KMM)

Index

Knight, L.F., 36, 37, 41
Knott, W.T., 101
K'tut Tantri. *See* Walker, Muriel Stewart
Kuala Lumpur, 2, 7, 8, 41, 104
Kuomintang, 21, 24, 48, 50, 54n7, 81, 118, 124

L

Labour Day rallies, 117, 135
Lai Teck, Secretary General, Communist Party of Malaya, 50, 54n9, 112, 115–16, 122, 124, 136–38
Langworthy, H.B., 27–28, 51
Larby, K.B., 6
Layard, Margaret Capel, 7–8
Leach, Lionel, 97n4
League against Imperialism, 69, 70
Lee Kuan Yew, 104
Lee Soong, 122, 125, 131
Leighton, E., 99
Liaison between Johor and Singapore Special Branches, 8, 11n11
Lim Ah Liang, 112, 116, 123–24
Linggadjati Agreement, 57–58
Livingstone, D.N., 6
Lloyd, Hugh Pugh, 94
Local Security Officer (LSO), 3, 8

M

MacArthur, Douglas, 14

MacDonald, Malcolm, 26, 27, 53n5, 59, 90, 93, 98n10
  colonial office telegram to, 35–37
  conference convened by, 47–48
  on Dalley's report, 51–52
Madoc, Guy C., 30n4
Malaya, 83, 88. *See also* Indonesian encroachment into Malaya
  Adat Perpateh, 67–68
  British colonial rule, 46, 56, 81, 88
  communism in, 47, 48, 73–75
  Communist Party in, 73
  Ducroux, Joseph, 71–73
  immigration control, 88–89
  independence declaration for, 57
  and Indonesian "Communists", 61
  Islamic political party in, 79
  Kesatuan Melayu Muda, 60–61
  left-wing parties, 46, 56, 59–60, 74, 75
  1926 Revolution in Java, 64–67, 71
  rubber smallholders, 47
  Singapore and, 38, 40, 57, 59, 72–73, 75, 80
  South Seas Communist Party, 70–71, 86n15
  Soviet Republic in, 77
  Tan Malaka's report on, 63–64

Malayan Campaign, 2, 22
Malayan Chinese Association
  (MCA), 54n9
Malayan Communist Party
  (MCP), 14, 15, 19, 29,
  47–52, 110–38
Malayan Democratic Union
  (MDU), 48, 117
Malayan Emergency (1948–60),
  7, 29, 81–84
*Malayan Establishment Staff List
  1948*, 5–6, 10n5
Malayan Indian Congress (MIC),
  48, 49
Malayan People's Anti-Japanese
  Army (MPAJA), 14, 23, 61,
  111, 112, 133
Malayan People's Democratic
  Union, 117
Malayan People's United Front,
  117
"Malayan Revolution", 77
Malayan Security Service (MSS),
  1, 13, 26, 106
  archives, ix
  Charter, 4–5, 39–41
  deficiencies in, 15
  gazetted officers, 5, 6
  gazetted officers staff list 1948,
  6
  main functions of, 40
  shortage of staff, xi, 8
  staff, 4, 6–8
Malayan Special Branch, 63

*Malaya's Secret Police 1945–60:
  The Role of the Special Branch
  in the Malayan Emergency*
  (Comber), 95
"Malay Communist Party",
  75–76
Malay Nationalist Party (MNP),
  48, 60–61, 80, 83, 117,
  121–22
Malay secret societies (*Kongsi
  Gelap Melayu*), 15–16
Manchuria, 26, 29
Mann, Tom, 68
Mary Rose motor launch, 24, 25
Mathieson, D., 29
MCA. *See* Malayan Chinese
  Association (MCA)
McLean, J.M., 14
MCP. *See* Malayan Communist
  Party (MCP)
MDU. *See* Malayan Democratic
  Union (MDU)
Mecca Pilgrimage, 40
"Memorandum of Instruction", 36
Menzies, Stewart, 96
MI5 (British domestic
  intelligence service), 2, 8,
  38, 40, 41
  disagreement with MSS,
  36–37, 42
MI6 (British foreign intelligence
  service), 38, 96
MIC. *See* Malayan Indian
  Congress (MIC)

Index

Minns, F.G., 101
Min Sheng Pau, 82
Min Yuen (People's Movement), 49–50
Missouri, USS, 14
MNP. *See* Malay Nationalist Party (MNP)
Moeso Soebakat, 75
Morgan, K.S., 25, 29
Morris, N.G., 6, 7, 91–92, 93, 99
Morton, John Percival (Jack), 39, 43n3
Mountbatten, Louis, 14
MPAJA. *See* Malayan People's Anti-Japanese Army (MPAJA)
MPAJA Ex-Servicemen's Association, 49, 112, 119
MSS. *See* Malayan Security Service (MSS)
Mulock, G.F.A., 24, 25
Mustapha Hussain, 57

N

Nan Chiau Girls' High School, 22
Nanyang Communist Party. *See* South Seas Communist Party
Nanyang Normal School, 22
Nathan, S.R., President of Singapore, vii–viii, xiii
Netherlands Steamship Co., 62
Newboult, Alexander, 94
New Democratic Youth League (Ikatan Pemudah Tanah Ayer), 49, 115, 119, 131
1926 Revolution in Java, 64–67, 71
Noulens, Hilaire, 71

O

Onn bin Ja'afar, 54n7
Onraet, René H. de S., 9n2, 71
Osprey motor launch, 24

P

Palmer, Sydney, 28
Palestine Police, 27–28
Pan Malayan Federation of Trade Unions (PMFTU), 125, 132
PAP. *See* People's Action Party (PAP)
PARI. *See* Partai Republikan Indonesia (PARI)
Partai Komunis Indonesia (PKI), 46, 66, 69, 73–76, 82–83, 86n14
Partai Republikan Indonesia (PARI), 72, 75
Peace Preservation Army (Tentera Keslamat Rakjat), 57
Pemoeda Rahasia Indonesia (Indonesia Youth Corps), 57
People's Action Party (PAP), 54n9, 55
Perak State Council, 16

Percival, Arthur Ernest, 2, 17, 24, 26
Pham Ngoc Tach, 126
Phoenix Park, 37, 47, 53n5
PIJ. See Political Intelligence Journal (PIJ)
Pilehan Timor, 69, 70
PKI. *See* Partai Komunis Indonesia (PKI)
PMFTU. *See* Pan Malayan Federation of Trade Unions
"Political Intelligence Bureau", 27
Political Intelligence Journal (PIJ), 8, 39, 58
Puhalo, D., 131

Q
Quixley, R.W., 6

R
Rashid Mydin. *See* Abdul Rashid bin Maidin
Recruit to Revolution: Adventure and Politics during the Indonesian Struggle for Independence (Coast), 91
Red Labour Union, 77
Renville Agreement, 58
Report of the Police Mission to Malaya (1950), 95
Ritchie, Neil, 94
RMS *Empress of Asia*, 23
Rotterdam Lloyd Co., 62

Round Table Conference, 58
Russian Army, 26
Ryves, H.T.B., 6

S
secret societies
 Chinese secret societies, 14, 24
 Malay secret societies (*Kongsi Gelap Melayu*), 15–16
Security and Intelligence Division (SID), 89, 97n3, 105
Security Intelligence Far East (SIFE), 7, 9, 35, 41, 89, 93, 110. *See also* SIFE Charter
Semaoen, 62
Serge le Franc, 71–73
Serpell, Michael F., 39
Seruan Azhar, 69, 70
Sharkey, Lance, 126
Shaw, Alexander Nicholas, x, 9n2
Sheppard, Mubin, 8, 11n12, 17–18, 31n10
SHLU. *See* Singapore Harbour Labour Union
Short, Anthony, 12n15, 15, 30n5, 81
SID. *See* Security and Intelligence Division (SID)
SIFE. *See* Security Intelligence Far East (SIFE)
SIFE Charter, 37

Heads/SIFE, 39
  text of, 38–39
Sillitoe, Percy, 9, 35, 37, 40, 43n9, 94
Singapore
  Chinese population of, 104
  communism in, 48
  external intelligence service, 105
  Lee Kuan Yew, 104
  Malaya and, 38, 40, 57, 59, 72–73, 75, 80
  opium from Indonesia, 90, 92
  post-war situation in, 13–14
  Security and Intelligence Division, 89, 97n3
Singapore Federation of Trade Unions, 82, 125, 134, 135
"Singapore Fortress Defence Scheme", 2
Singapore Harbour Board, 123, 133
Singapore Harbour Labour Union (SHLU), 132, 134
Singapore Special Branch, 64, 68, 69–71, 99–101, 105
Singapore Town Committee, 116
Soeara Boeroeh Malaya, 73
South Seas Communist Party, 70–71, 86n15
Soviet Union, 45, 46, 69
Stockwell, A.J., 90, 97n4
Sukarno, 57, 84, 89, 91
Sultan, HMS, 25

Sutan Jenain, 61
Sym, H.B., 25, 29

T

Taman Budiman: Memoirs of an Unorthodox Civil Servant (Sheppard), 8
Tan Cheng Lock, 135
Tan Chin Tuan, 18–19
Tan Kah Kee, 19, 21–22
Tan Kan, 132, 137
Tan Malaka, 61–64, 72–73, 75
Tan Peng, 126
Tentera Keslamat Rakjat (Peace Preservation Army), 57
Teo Yuen Foo, 74
Thistlewaite, Richard, 39
Thomas, Shenton, 17, 19
Triad and Tabut: A Study of the Origin and Diffusion of Chinese and Mohamedan Secret Societies in the Malay Peninsula AD 1800–1935 (Wynne), 16, 29
Tunku Abdul Rahman, 32, 104
23rd British Indian Infantry Division, 57, 84

U

UMNO. *See* United Malays National Organisation (UMNO)
Unification Committee, 78

Union of Indonesian Seamen, 61–62
United Malays National Organisation (UMNO), 49, 54n7, 82
UN Security Council, 58
USS *Missouri*, 14
Ustaz Abu Bakar al-Baqir, 79, 80, 87n23

V
Vanguard Weekly, 82
van Mook, Hubertus, 58
"Voice of Malayan Labour", 74

W
Walker, Muriel Stewart, 91
Wataniah, 61

WFDY. *See* World Federation of Democratic Youth
WFTU. *See* World Federation of Trade Unions (WFTU)
Winterborn, P. Hugh, 39, 47
Woolnough, H.J., 6, 100
Wootton, A.N., 25
World Federation of Democratic Youth (WFDY), 131
World Federation of Trade Unions (WFTU), 68–70
Wu Tien Wang, 49
Wylie, Ian S., 6, 50, 99
Wynne, M.L., 16, 25, 29, 30n9

Y
Yong Mun Cheong, 58, 85n5
Young, Courtney, 39

ABOUT THE AUTHOR

Dr Leon Comber is a Visiting Senior Fellow at the ISEAS – Yusof Ishak Institute, Singapore. His interest in Malaysia and Singapore extends from the time he first landed as a Major with the returning British/Indian forces as part of "Operation Zipper" through the surf at Morib Beach on the west coast of Malaya following the Japanese surrender at the end of WWII. Thereafter, he served for many years as a Chinese-speaking Special Branch officer in the Malayan Police dealing with political, security, and operational intelligence during the First Malayan Emergency. After leaving the Special Branch he had a distinguished career in book publishing, and was the Managing Director of Heinemann Asia, a subsidiary of Heinemann Educational Books, London, and the Publisher of the University of Hong Kong Press. He has a BA (Hons.), SOAS, University of London; an MA (Comparative Asian Studies), University of Hong Kong; an MBA (Distinction), University of East Asia, Macau; and a PhD from Monash University, Australia. His languages are Cantonese, Mandarin, and Malay, with some Hindi.

Among his recent books are *Singapore Chronicles: Japanese Occupation*; *Templer and the Road to Malayan Independence: The Man and his Time*; *Malaya's Secret Police 1945–60: The Role of the Special Branch in the Malayan Emergency*; and *Singapore Correspondent: Political Dispatches from Singapore (1958–1962)*.

Artist's impression of Lieutenant Colonel John Douglas Dalley, Commander, Dalforce, and Director, Malayan Security Service (MSS).
Image courtesy of ISD Heritage Centre, Singapore.

The end of the troopship *Empress of Asia* after a determined Japanese bombing attack on 5 February 1942, just eight kilometres from Singapore. The ship sailed from Liverpool in November 1941 carrying troops and supplies for Africa, Bombay and Singapore. The supplies intended for Dalley's "Dalforce" went down with it. Singapore surrendered ten days later.
Image courtesy of Australian War Memorial, ref. P01604.001.

Photograph from the Straits Settlement's Police Officers' Mess.
Major K.S. Morgan, Head, Japanese Section of the Singapore Special Branch, can be seen in the second row, fifth from the left.
Image courtesy of ISD Heritage Centre, Singapore.

G.C. Madoc, former Dy. Director MSS and Director of Intelligence, Malaya (appointed in 1954).
Image courtesy of Singapore Police Force.

Nigel G. Morris, Acting Dy. Director MSS and Commissioner of Police, Singapore, 1953-57.
Image courtesy of ISD Heritage Centre, Singapore.

Alan E.G. Blades, Assistant Director MSS and Commissioner of Police, Singapore, 1958-63.
Image courtesy of ISD Heritage Centre, Singapore.

CONFIDENTIAL B.A. M.I. 9(JAP) N° 49254 A

WRITE IN BLOCK CAPITAL LETTERS IN PENCIL

No. ? Rank LT. COL Surname DALLEY
Christian Names JOHN DOUGLAS Decorations
Ship (R.N. U.S.N. or Merchant Navy) Unit & Div. (Army) GENERAL LIST COMMANDED DALFORCE IN MALAYA
Squadron and Command (R.A.F. A.A.F.)
Date of Birth DEC. 6th 1900 Date of Enlistment DECEMBER 1941
Private Address and Telephone No. MARSTON HOUSE, MARSTON MAGNA, SOMERSET.
Place and Date of Original Capture (Aircrew R.A.F. to give place and date of a/c crash) 17th FEB. 1942. AT SEA.

1. What camps, detachments or hospitals were you in ? Give dates and names of the British Camp Leaders, Detachment (or Block) Leaders or, in the case of hospitals, the Senior British Medical Officers.

Camp or Hospital	Dates	Camp Leader	Detachment or Block Leader (if any)
MUNTOK, BANKA	17/2/42 - 7/3/42	AIR-COM. MODIN	
TANJONG PRIOK GLODOK	APRIL MAY 1942	S.CAPT. NOBLE	
TANJONG PRIOK (BATAVIA AREA)	MAY 1942 - SEPT 1943	COL. CM. LAKE	
CHANGI	SEPT 1943 - OCT. 1943		
SHIRAKAWA, TAIWAN	NOV. 1943 - FEB 1945		
MIATA, JAPAN	MARCH 1945 - APRIL 1945		
MUKDEN	APRIL 1945 - SEPT 1945		

2. ESCAPES OR ATTEMPTED ESCAPES. (Additional paper will be supplied on request if required).

(a) Give full description and approx. date of each attempt you made to escape, showing how you left the camp, and from which camp each attempt was made. State whether there was an air-raid in progress at the time or not. If an escape was made from a train or vehicle the approx. speed and how it was guarded should be included.

7th March 1942, left Muntok. Went through the lines at night and travelled by land and sea to Java. Recaptured there on 24th April 1942. 24 Apl
b. Made several attempts from camps in Java but attempts neither detected by Japanese nor successful. (Details of escape)

(b) Were you physically fit when you made these attempts ?
Yes

(c) Give Regimental particulars of anyone who accompanied you on each attempt.
L/A.E.ENO, GENERAL LIST (attached to Dalforce in Malaya)
L/Seaman T. PARSONS
Sergt. K. WHARTON, A.I.F.
What happened to them?
Recaptured on 24th April 1942. Present whereabouts unknown. 24 Apl

(d) Give briefly your experiences during periods of freedom.
Just a long chase on land by bands of natives & Japanese. Acquired a small boat & got away to sea. Landed in Java & given away by natives.
(C). No suitable boat available.
(e). How were you recaptured and on what date?
Landed in Java and immediately surrounded by natives. Took arms from us & persuaded them not to kill us. Japanese arrived after being informed of our whereabouts by natives - 24th April 1942. 24 Apl P.T.O.

www.ingramcontent.com/pod-product-compliance
Lightning Source LLC
Chambersburg PA
CBHW051101230426
43667CB00013B/2393